MW00719356

BREAKING
THE
STRESS HABIT

A Modern Guide
To One-Minute Stress Management

by
Andrew G. Goliszek, Ph.D.

Carolina Press
Box 24906
Winston-Salem, NC 27114

Copyright 1987 Andrew G. Goliszek, Ph.D.

All Rights Reserved. No part of this book may be reproduced or transmitted in any form or by any means, electronic or mechanical, including photocopying, recording, or by an information storage and retrieval system—except by a reviewer who many quote brief passages in a review to be printed in a magazine or newspaper—without permission in writing from the publisher. For information, please contact Carolina Press, P.O. Box 24906, Winston-Salem, NC 27114.

Although the authors and publishers have made every effort to ensure the accuracy and completeness of information contained in this book, we assume no responsibility for errors, inaccuracies, omissions, or any inconsistency herein. Any slights of people or organizations are unintentional. Readers should use their own judgment for application to their individual problems.

Library of Congress Cataloging-in-Publication Data

Goliszek, Andrew G.
  Breaking the Stress Habit

  Bibliography: p.
  Includes index.
  1. Stress (Psychology) 2. Stress (Physiology)
3. Relaxation. 4. Meditation. I. Title.
  BF575.S75G6   1988   158'.1   87-25014
  ISBN 0-9616475-2-3
  ISBN 0-9616475-3-1 (pbk.)

ATTENTION HEALTH PROFESSIONALS, COR-PORATIONS, UNIVERSITIES, GOVERNMENT AGENCIES: Quantity discounts are available on bulk purchases of this book for patient, educational, business, or promotional use. For information, please contact our Special Sales Department, CAROLINA PRESS, Box 24906, Winston-Salem, NC 27114 or call (919) 760–0944.

Second printing 1988.
Printed and bound in the United States of America

DEDICATION

To my wife Kathy and our children Jennifer, David, and Paul. Their love, patience, and support helped me through the many long hours it took to write and complete this book.

ACKNOWLEDGMENTS

My appreciation and thanks to Kathy Goliszek, Judy Perrault, and Ted Getchel for taking the time to read through the initial manuscript and offer insightful comments and critiques.

I would also like to thank Marilyn Ross and the staff of About Books Inc. for their expert advice and support. Their valuable suggestions added to the scope of this book and their editorial comments greatly enhanced both its quality and substance.

TABLE OF CONTENTS

Appendices

PART I

STRESS
COPING AND
MANAGEMENT

INTRODUCTION

It's been called the "Disease of the Twentieth Century"; it's believed to cause more ailments than anything else known to modern medicine. And whether we realize it or not, for most of us, it's become a habit we just can't seem to kick.

For years, doctors have been warning us that stress is harmful to our health; and the latest evidence clearly shows that being exposed to stress on a regular basis can trigger major diseases like cancer, hypertension, and coronary heart disease. Deaths from illnesses linked to stress have been growing at an alarming rate, and it's not surprising that countries having the most stressful lifestyles are also the ones with the greatest increase in stress-related deaths. So, with all the bad news about stress, why is it so hard for us to break the stress habit and just learn to relax? The answer may be that we don't treat our stress responses the same way we treat any other habit we acquire and get used to. As a result, stress has become something we accept. We learn to live with it.

Few of us are born worriers, and even fewer of us are naturally prone to anxiety or tension until we begin to develop the habit of responding that way. For most of us, this happens early in life and, therefore, changing our ingrained behavior isn't easy and takes time. But like any behavior pattern that needs changing, our stress response patterns can be easily modified so that stress no longer makes us physically or emotionally sick, but instead makes us feel challenged and invigorated.

How do we go about breaking the stress habit so that the quality of our lives is better? First, by learning what stress is, what it does to us, and why we respond to it the way we do. Second, by learning to recognize stress symptoms and linking those symptoms with daily events in our lives. Third, by making gradual changes in our behavior patterns and attitudes. And fourth, by learning quick and simple stress management relaxation techniques and exercises that can be done anytime with little effort.

This book is presented in a sequence so that certain principles of stress management build on one another. The first chapter, which explains what stress is and how it affects us, is important for understanding coping strategies and stress management techniques discussed later on. If we don't know what's going on inside us, we can't manage it. The next few chapters describe ways to recognize stress symptoms, things we can do to change our attitudes and behavior patterns that cause stress, and practical methods we can use to turn stressful events into positive and rewarding experiences. The final chapters explain and give examples of various stress management techniques—from muscle relaxation to meditation.

All these techniques can be mastered with a little practice and used any place at anytime. "One-minute stress management" simply means that, with these techniques and coping strategies, we'll be able to start the stress relief process within 60 seconds. This is very important, considering how busy our daily lives are and how difficult it can be to make time for even something as simple as relaxation.

All our perceptions, our responses, and our reactions to stress are initiated during the first few seconds of a stress encounter. What we do during the next sixty seconds determines how our body will deal with that encounter and whether or not we succeed in developing habits that help us manage stress in a way that minimizes illness and disease. Every stress management exercise, technique, and strategy should begin during those first sixty seconds. Whether we practice relaxation techniques, learn time management skills, or use coping strategies, the decision to do something during that first minute of stress is critical if we want to condition ourselves to become "one-minute stress managers." The sooner we put our one-minute stress management skills into practice, the sooner we condition ourselves to respond automatically and appropriately whenever stress occurs.

Because we've developed an attitude that everything needs to be done quickly and effectively, most of us are indifferent or turned off to stress management. Many relaxation techniques take more work than they're worth. This book has been written with just that in mind. Hopefully, after reading the chapters and practicing the techniques and exercises, you'll discover that stress management has become a normal but important part of your life. And as you see and feel the tremendous effect that stress relief has on the quality of your life, you'll realize as never before that feeling good is really easy. It's never more than a minute away.

1

Stress:
What It Is
and What It Does

Throughout history, each new generation has created and been exposed to its own kind of stress. Today, stress might be the result of having to deal with high-tech careers, fast paced business transactions, divorce, or social and family problems. But long before we ever knew what stress was all about, our ancestors depended on the stress response for life itself—to flee from predators, to fight enemies, and to survive in a hostile world that left little room for the weak and helpless. The world at that time was divided into the responders and the nonresponders. Those who were able to respond to life-threatening events survived and passed their genes onto the next generation. Those who couldn't eventually disappeared. With each new generation, the ability to respond to stress grew until it evolved into the amazingly efficient and complex set of reactions that are such a mixed blessing today. On the one hand, we need to respond to stress or die; on the other hand, we also need to control the way we respond to stress or else we become sick and eventually die. Somewhere along the line, we developed into superresponders, able to react immediately to almost any life situation, yet unable to control the way we react. As a result, stress wove its way into every aspect of our society and has become another part of our lives we take for granted.

Our ancestors probably responded to stress only when they had to. We respond to stress automatically—mostly out of habit—to thousands of events, situations, and crises throughout our lives. Over the course of history, we've become a civilization of overresponders. Our ability to respond has developed to such an extent that the smallest dilemma can trigger a major reaction; the most insignificant event can send us into a frenzy. What began eons ago as a vital defense mechanism is today the leading cause of disease and illness in the modern world. The origin of stress has its roots in our primeval past. Our continual adaptation to stress has some experts wondering if we've adapted a little too well and stepped beyond our ability to control the forces within us. Let's look at those forces now and see exactly what happens to us during the stressful moments in our lives.

The Stress Response

You walk into your office Monday morning and see a stack of work that looks like it's going to take a month to do. Something happens inside of you—you can feel it and you can sense it. Almost from the start, your body automatically begins to respond without your even being aware of it. If you're an overresponder, your response quickly builds until your body signals the stress with some kind of symptom like pain, nausea, or anxiety and lets you know something's wrong. If you're a slow responder, you may not get the signal until you get home that evening or after you've gone to bed. But whether you're an overresponder or a slow responder, exactly the same things happen inside your body. Figure 1a illustrates the series of chain reactions that are supposed to protect our body from further harm and help us recover from the stress we've encountered.

The word stress has been borrowed from engineering. In engineering, stress is defined as any external force that produces a strain on a structure. The amount of strain depends on the magnitude of the stress and the properties of the structure.

In psychology, the external force is a "stressor" and the strain it produces is referred to as stress. And like the strain in engineering, the amount of strain we're able to handle depends on the amount and magnitude of stress and the extent of our coping abilities. In order to understand the concepts of stress management, we need to recognize the three elements involved in stress. These are:

1. The Stressor, which is the event or situation that puts us on alert and gets us ready to respond.
2. Stress, which is a condition or state of imbalance between the stressful situation and our ability or capacity to cope with that situation.
3. Stress Reactions, which are the physical and emotional responses resulting from exposure to stressful situations.

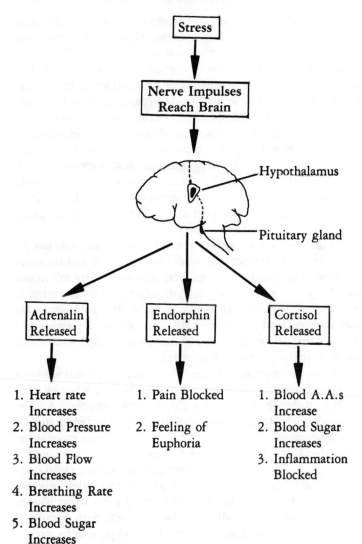

Figure 1a
Physical reactions of the Stress Response

Any stressful event—physical or emotional—sends a signal to an area of our brain called the Hypothalamus. Once the Hypothalamus is stimulated, it does two things: (1) it sends nerve impulses to the adrenal glands located on top of our kidneys, and (2) it sends a chemical message to the pituitary gland located at the base of our brain. Stimulation of these two glands prepares our body for "fight or flight" (we either stay and fight or we run away) and provides us with the biological ammunition we need to withstand most stressful encounters. When the stress response is initiated, the stage is then set for a host of other physical reactions that kick in and are responsible for making us feel and act the way we do during stress. The three main reactions that occur during stress are: (1) a surge of adrenalin, (2) a discharge of cortisol, and (3) a release of endorphin.

Adrenalin—the main stress chemical—makes our heart rate go up. The increase in heart rate raises blood pressure and increases blood flow, which in turn brings extra oxygen to every cell in our body. Oxygen is nature's purest fuel, driving biochemical reactions, regulating blood gases like carbon dioxide, and pumping extra energy into our system. Without the increased blood pressure and blood flow that deliver extra oxygen, our ability to fight stress (or an aggressor) would be seriously impaired.

Adrenalin also increases glucose or blood sugar, and this release is perhaps the single most important event that happens when we meet a sudden challenge. Because it's the starting compound for the body's energy supply, glucose is absolutely critical for producing the extra energy molecules needed during prolonged stress encounters. During stress, the stored form of glucose called glycogen is converted to pure glucose molecules through a remarkable chain reaction that produces some 100 million glucose molecules for every molecule of adrenalin released. This reaction gives us an instant source of energy by literally flooding our cells with enormous amounts of glucose only seconds after we've responded to stress.

Cortisol—produced by the cortex or outer layer of the adrenal gland—causes an increase in blood amino acids as well as an increase in blood sugar. Since many types of stress lead to tissue damage, amino acids (the building materials from which protein is made) are crucial for the proper recovery of injured or damaged tissues. The increase in glucose adds to the already abundant supply of circulating glucose molecules produced by adrenalin and multiplies our energy reserves even more.

Endorphin—a morphinelike substance—is produced in the brain and is several hundred times more potent than morphine itself. It's released immediately from the brain during any kind of stress, painful stimuli, exercise, or emergency situation and is part of our body's natural tranquilizing system. Long distance runners, for example, experience a "runner's high" because the pain and stress of long exercise stimulates the release of endorphin. Serious athletes, who get that endorphin surge more often than nonathletes or part-time athletes, get a feeling of euphoria that can become addictive and lead to mild exercise withdrawal. Since the discovery of endorphin in 1975, we now know that both physical and emotional stress can be greatly lessened through regular exercise programs and that people who never exercise are much more susceptible to the negative effects of stress reactions.

The unifying concept of stress is that it doesn't matter what the source of stress is—the results are always the same. The businessperson who is pressured by deadlines, the wife whose husband just died, the student who goes to an exam unprepared, and the patient who finds out he has a serious illness all experience different stressors, yet all respond in the same biological manner. In essence, our stress response is nonspecific, meaning that it occurs regardless of which factors are producing it. These nonspecific responses have evolved so that we won't have to worry about what to respond to and what to ignore. We respond to everything because our body doesn't allow any stress-producing factors to get by our biological defense shields. This automatic reaction which brings our body back to a state of normalcy is the principle element of stress and the main driving force behind the stress response.

Stress Rating Scale

Although we all respond to stress events in exactly the same way, the degree to which we respond and the extent to which we're affected depend on the intensity and duration. And because we all perceive stress events differently, what's upsetting for one person may concern someone else very little.

There are certain events, however, that seem to be universally stressful for people throughout the world. Drs. Thomas H. Holmes and Richard H. Rahe, psychiatrists at the University of Washington Medical School, have developed a scale that ranks various stressors according to their intensity and severity. Dr. Holmes's research indicates that experiencing a stress event point score of 300 or more during any one year is dangerous and should be cause for concern. According to the doctors, even pleasant changes or experiences can create stress and make us more susceptible to resulting illness. The following events, both good and bad, make up the scale of stressful events:

Events	Scale of Impact
Death of spouse	100
Divorce	73
Marital separation	65
Jail term	63
Death of close family member	63
Personal injury or illness	53
Marriage	50
Fired at work	47
Marital reconciliation	45
Retirement	45
Change in health of family member	44
Pregnancy	40
Sexual difficulties	39
Gain of new family member	39
Business readjustment	39
Change in financial state	38
Death of a close friend	37
Change to different line of work	36
Change in number of arguments with spouse	35
Foreclosure of mortgage or loan	30
Change in responsibilities at work	29
Son or daughter leaving home	29
Trouble with in-laws	29
Outstanding personal achievement	28
Wife begins or stops work	26
Begin or end school	26
Change in living conditions	25
Revision of personal habits	24
Trouble with boss	23
Change in work hours or conditions	20
Change in residence	20
Change in schools	20
Change in recreation	19

Change in church activities	19
Change in social activities	18
Change in sleeping habits	16
Change in number of family get-togethers	15
Change in eating habits	15
Vacation	13
Christmas	12
Minor violations of the law	11

There's no easy way to predict how much stress is too much because stressors often work together to magnify our response and increase the intensity of reactions. The stress response, then, is really a group of reactions set off during any kind of stress event. Other factors, such as diet, lifestyle, and heredity also come into play and complicate the picture even more. These other factors multiply the effects of our stress response, intensifying it and combining with it to increase the likelihood of disease. As a short-term defense mechanism, the stress response is without question a necessary and important part of our lives. Our goal, however, should be to modify that stress response so it's no longer a spontaneous overreaction, but rather a natural, stimulating part of our stress-fighting reserves!

Stress and Immunity

Immunity simply means having resistance to foreign particles or substances that enter the body. Without immunity, our body wouldn't be able to combat the viruses, bacteria, and other microorganisms that constantly invade our system. So, in order to protect us from these invaders, we have at our disposal a complex "immune response" that involves special cells called lymphocytes or white blood cells and NK or Natural Killer cells. Both the lymphocytes and the Natural Killer cells attack foreign bodies and are vital in our fight against infection, illness, and disease. Stress has a tremendously negative effect on our ability to fight illness and disease because it suppresses our immune system's capacity to produce and maintain lymphocytes and NK cells. Figure 1b illustrates what happens to our immune response during stress.

In general, the two ingredients necessary to develop an illness or disease are an invading foreign substance and a lowered resistance. Physical and/or emotional stress alter, and may in fact shut down, the immune response. This lowers our resistance and makes us more prone to attack by everything from common cold viruses to cancer

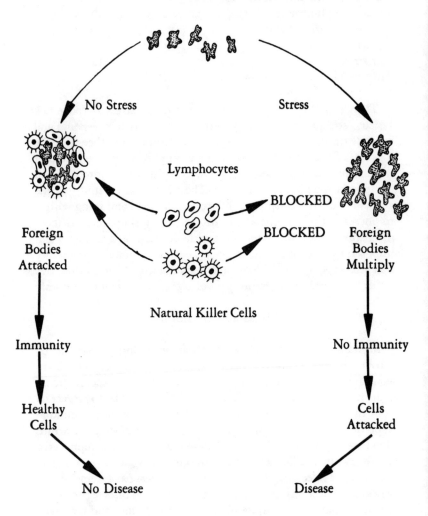

Figure 1b
Effects of stress on the Immune Response.

cells. One theory of cancer growth suggests that everyone at some point in their life develops a cancer. The difference between those who fall victim to it and those who don't is that victims become extra vulnerable due to a decreased immune response. When this happens, the cancer, instead of being attacked and destroyed by Natural Killer cells, is allowed to grow uncontrollably because Natural Killer cells are inactivated during stress. Susceptible individuals may be the unlucky ones who become stressed more easily and more often increasing their chances of eventually succumbing to some form of cancer growth.

During stress, our lymphocytes are also depressed, leaving us open to all sorts of health problems because letting our immune guard down for even an instant leads to a massive invasion of foreign bodies. Without lymphocytes to attack these foreign bodies, they become free to reproduce uncontrollably and cause infection or search out and destroy healthy cells. A change in our immune response can drastically limit our ability to fight even the most insignificant illness. And it can certainly trigger the onset of major diseases.

Stress-Related Illnesses and Diseases

Some of the main diseases now believed to be at least partially blamed on long-term exposure to stress are coronary heart disease, hypertension, kidney disease, and arteriosclerosis. But during the last decade, a host of illnesses including chronic backache, gastritis, migraine headaches, psoriasis, eczema, cold sores, shingles, hives, and ulcers have also been closely linked to stress. The stress itself doesn't cause the illness or disease but helps bring it about because it increases our susceptibility by decreasing our immunity. Once the source of stress is found and eliminated, minor illnesses usually disappear until stress is encountered again.

How do we know it's stress and not something else causing many of our health problems? Some examples will illustrate how stress is closely linked to health problems and that there's little doubt about stress being a major force in the disease process.

In many parts of the world, where stress isn't a normal part of life, coronary heart disease is very uncommon. Once people in these areas are exposed to the stresses of modern society, they become as susceptible as anyone else. Italians in one Pennsylvania community, for example, had a a very low death rate from heart disease even though they lived on a very high-fat diet. When the community became increasingly urbanized, the death rate from heart disease gradually increased until it became similar to every other community in the area.

Other studies have shown that heart disease is linked to cholesterol levels which increase with stress. Accountants, for example, have higher cholesterol levels during the hectic tax season, students have higher cholesterol levels during exam weeks, and people losing their jobs have much higher cholesterol levels that later drop when they find work. Even minor nervous tension and anxiety, if allowed to continue long enough, have a big effect on blood cholesterol levels and on the susceptibility to heart problems.

Researchers at Brown and Yale Universities found that a number of men who were about to lose their jobs developed accelerated clogging of the arteries, while others developed ulcers, swollen joints, patchy bald spots, diabetes, and gout. In another study done at Cape Kennedy, workers who knew that their jobs would be ending right after a successful moon landing had a 50 percent higher than normal death rate from sudden cardiac death. In both cases, concern about imminent job loss created an excessive stress response which caused disease-producing reactions.

Hypertension, or high blood pressure, is the most common cardiovascular disease and affects over 30 million Americans each year. We know that smoking, obesity, alcohol consumption, kidney disorders, high salt intake, and heredity can all raise blood pressure. But now we also know that stress can be a major factor in triggering the onset of at least 20 percent of all hypertension cases. The stress of factory noise, for example, has been closely linked to high blood pressure in factory workers exposed to prolonged, daily noise; flood victims experiencing devastating property and financial loss have developed permanent high blood pressure during their recovery periods; and executives in their early 30's, who were chronically angry and hostile but who supressed their anger and hostility because they couldn't express themselves, developed high blood pressure before they reached their 50's.

Even school children are susceptible to high blood pressure when they're placed in stressful situations. In one study of 9 to 16-year-olds, it was discovered that a routine act like reading out loud in front of classmates caused significant elevations in blood pressure. In another study, done in the Philippines, it was found that children who were placed in a lower academic achievement class had a much greater incidence of high blood pressure than children placed in a higher achievement class because of the stigma placed on lower scholastic ability in a society that demands scholastic excellence. These studies show that it's not only adults but also children who fall victim to hypertension as a direct result of stressful events in their lives.

In many cases, skin problems such as eczema, psoriasis, and shingles have been cured by using stress management techniques since many skin diseases result from emotional stress. Because our skin is actually an entire system in itself, it can sense emotional changes and is often the first part of our body to respond and reveal stress through symptoms such as hives, rashes, blotches, etc. Through a complex nerve system, the skin transmits subtle messages and signals our body to react whenever our brain senses some kind of negative feedback. Techniques like relaxation training, biofeedback, psychotherapy, and hypnosis have completely eliminated skin disorders in patients who had serious stress-related problems.

One of the best examples of how stress can be linked to disease is shown from the records of twenty-five thousand World War II POW's who were examined for six years following their liberation or escape from prison. Besides mortality rates being much higher than normal, the veterans who endured the greatest amount of stress during their imprisonment had seven times as many hospital admissions for a variety of ailments and major diseases. The amount of doctor visits and the degree of illness were almost entirely dependent on the extent of stress suffered.

Until recently, most illnesses were attributed to things like diet, heredity, environment, and lifestyle. Not so anymore. The evidence now points in a new direction and links stress to a wide range of illnesses from headaches and ulcers to multiple sclerosis and cancer. Many of these illnesses and diseases can be controlled because our immune system is directly tied in with our feelings, emotions, attitudes, and thought patterns. By learning to change attitudes and control thought patterns, we can help keep our immune system from working overtime and give it a chance to do what it does best—to act as a first line of defense against anything it sees as a threat to our health and well-being. Managing stress is without a doubt one of the single most important elements in ensuring that that defense is there and ready when we need it most!

General Adaptation Syndrome

We've all heard expressions like "he's going to drive himself to an early grave," or "she's worrying herself to death." The reason individuals become more susceptible to disease in the long run is not only because their immune systems become impaired but because they experience a natural breakdown of all the systems in the body.

In 1926, a young medical student named Hans Selye noticed that patients in the early stages of various infectious diseases all had similar symptoms regardless of the type of infectious disease they had. At that time, no one recognized the significance of these symptoms because they were "nonspecific"—that is, they were common to all infectious diseases and, therefore, couldn't be used for diagnosis or treatment. This phenomenon of common signs and symptoms was tucked away in the back of Selye's mind for the next ten years. Then in 1936, while searching for a new hormone in cattle ovaries, Selye discovered three sets of responses that occurred whenever he injected animals with any toxic substance: (1) the adrenal glands enlarged; (2) the lymph nodes and other lymphocyte-producing structures shrank; and (3) severe bleeding ulcers appeared in the stomach and intestines. The phenomenon of nonspecific signs and symptoms he had noticed ten years earlier as a medical student was happening again! He called these common stress responses the General Adaptation Syndrome and proposed the idea that certain changes taking place within our body during stress disrupt normal physiologic mechanisms and cause diseases such as arteriosclerosis, hypertension, ulcers, diabetes, kidney disease, and arthritis. According to Selye, "stress is a condition which leads to many abnormally-induced changes in our body and causes wear and tear to our entire system."

During the course of the General Adaptation Syndrome, diagrammed in figure 1c, our body responds to continual stress in a negative way over a period of time because it can't maintain resistance indefinitely. When we're constantly exposed to stressful events that change the way our body normally functions, eventually something has to happen. What happens is that our body goes through several stages of intense physical activity until it can't keep up with the stress any longer. Once this occurs, our body loses its ability to fight off disease and begins to deteriorate rapidly. Let's look at what happens during the three stages of the General Adaptation Syndrome.

Stage 1. Alarm Reaction: Stress causes us to respond immediately with reactions that combat the stress. Because the immune system is initially depressed, our normal level of resistance is lowered at first and we become more susceptible to illness and disease. If the stress isn't very severe or long-lasting, we eventually bounce back and recover quickly.

Stage 2. Resistance: During prolonged stress exposure, we adapt to the stress, and there's actually a tendency for our resistance to increase above normal. Any organism gets used to certain conditions if the conditions are present long enough. Therein lies the danger. We begin to feel good, unaware that our body is still in a state of "stress resistance." Our body works overtime during this stage to keep us healthy, but at the same time loses its ability to keep up with the demand that stress is putting on it.

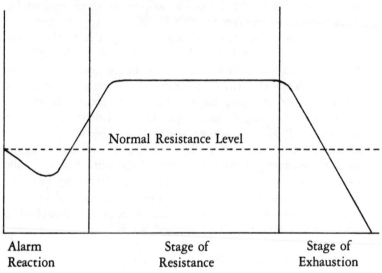

| Alarm | Stage of | Stage of |
| Reaction | Resistance | Exhaustion |

Figure 1c
General Adaptation Syndrome

Stage 3. Exhaustion: Because our body isn't able to maintain the long-term resistance needed to combat stress, there's eventually a sudden drop in our resistance followed by collapse. We can't say for sure when that happens since every individual has his or her own level of resistance and tolerance. But like any delicate machine, our body reaches a limit beyond which it can no longer function reliably. Our immunity breaks down. Our organ systems malfunction. And the fine-tuned mechanisms that drive life-giving reactions sputter and eventually shut down. We finally exhaust our stress-fighting reserves and succumb to what Selye called "diseases of adaptation."

"The three stages of the General Adaptation Syndrome," Selye said, "can be compared to childhood (low resistance and excessive responses), adulthood (during which the body adapts to most stimuli and becomes resistant), and old age (during which the body loses its adaptability and becomes exhausted)." Like everything in nature, human life cycles can be affected by outside stressors as a result of changes in our behaviors, attitudes, and perceptions. Any one of these can shift us into the later stages of resistance and make us more susceptible to the diseases of adaptation which account for many illnesses in younger people who live very stressed lives.

The General Adaptation Syndrome is thought to be the reason why stress is becoming such an abundant source of health problems. As our society becomes increasingly more complex, we're continually faced with new challenges that crop up faster more intensely than ever before. By changing the way our body normally functions, these stress challenges disrupt the natural balance crucial for well-being. They also increase our susceptibility to disease and subtract years from our lives by speeding up the body's aging process. Resistance is really the name of the game when we talk about disease, physical disability, or aging. Stress can virtually cripple our chances for extending or improving life! It does so by breaking down resistance and increasing the odds that all our bodily functions will eventually give out and fail us.

Stress Response as a Habit

Habits are defined as behavior patterns that become regular or spontaneous due to regular repetition. A habit increases in strength over time because it's really a kind of conditioned response that becomes ingrained in our subconscious and is released whenever a certain mental or environmental cue is given. Like any conditioned reflex or response, our response to stress is influenced by what we learn, how we act, and how often we do the things we do whenever we encounter stressful events. In essence, the stress response can be inhibited or enhanced through simple conditioning and become a habit as irritating and spontaneous as nail biting, foot tapping, or smoking. Figure 1d illustrates how stress can lead to a conditioning pattern that alters and shapes our stress response. Let's look at two common examples of how someone can develop or create a conditioned pattern that leads to spontaneous stress reactions.

John gets a new job and soon begins to get irritated at some of the things his boss says or does to him. In particular, John resents the

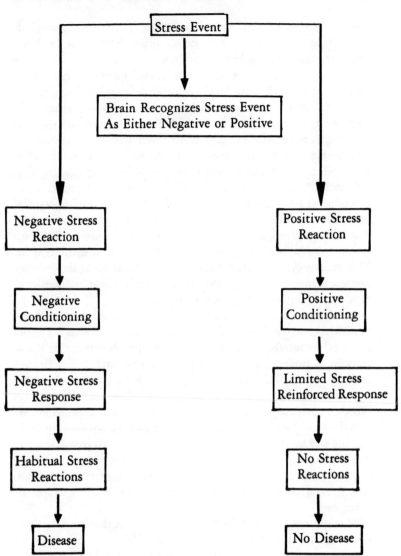

Figure 1d
Process of stress-induced conditioning & habit formation

way he's being treated, but since he needs the job, he can't do anything about it for fear of being fired. Each time he has a confrontation with his boss, John has a stress reaction. The stress reaction begins to come more easily and more quickly and is longer-lasting each time he has a confrontation. Before long, he begins to anticipate stress and gets a stress reaction without the confrontation. Now, John begins to feel as if he has no control over his situation because he gets upset even without his source of stress—his boss. He experiences negative reactions at home and on weekends by just thinking about his boss. These reactions, repeated over and over again, eventually condition John to react spontaneously whenever he consciously or even subconsciously thinks about his boss. The more he thinks about the stress, the more intensely he responds to it. And the more intensely he responds, the more conditioned he becomes to respond more easily to it the next time. This vicious cycle is a classic example of how the stress response can become a major habit that gets progressively worse and harder to break in a relatively short period of time.

Another very common example of a stress-related response habit is male secondary impotence. The reason stress plays such a major role in the overwhelming number of sexual problems is that sexual activity is under the influence of the autonomic or involuntary nervous system. Whenever a man gets aroused, nerve impulses from his brain cause blood vessels in the penis to dilate, allowing a flow of blood to enter the spongy tissue. At the same time, a special muscle called a sphincter contracts and prevents blood from flowing back. During any kind of stress, the sphincter muscle fails to contract and causes the penis to loss the blood needed for erection. Almost any kind of stressful event can cause this to happen, but in most cases, emotional stress and anxiety are the most common. Here's a specific example:

Harry comes home from work tired and still thinking about all the work he didn't get done that day. When he tries to have intercourse, he's still thinking about what he didn't get done at work or what he has to do the next day. Suddenly, he notices that for the first time he either can't get an erection or he can't maintain one. Without realizing it, he blames his failure completely on himself. The next evening, he thinks about whether he will fail again. He tries harder in order to make up for his last failure. And because of his anxiety, he undoubtedly fails again. The harder he tries, the more he fails and the deeper his conditioning becomes. Soon, the stress of performance anxiety is an ingrained, spontaneous stress habit that causes instant impotence whenever he thinks about sexual activity. Eventually, Harry begins to avoid intimacy and sexual contact altogether.

This vicious cycle is a typical pattern caused by a repetitive stressful event, and a classic example of how negative stress eventually creates a spontaneous stress reaction. The longer the habit is allowed to continue and intensify, the more ingrained it becomes. And because physical activities such as intercourse are mainly controlled by the autonomic nervous system, the conditioning process is more easily developed but much harder to break. The underlying power behind this conditioning process is our inability to recognize stress as the primary source of the problem in the first place.

From the moment we're born, we become creatures of habit. Our behavior is shaped by our environment, our parents, our siblings, our society, and our teachers. We learn to respond to certain events and situations in our lives because they represent either pleasure or displeasure, harmony or discord. And we use our habits to free our minds of routine tasks and simplify our day-to-day existence. By the time we reach adulthood, we'll have organized behavior patterns and developed habits that we'll use, in either a positive or negative way, for the rest of our lives. And before we die, we'll have accumulated thousands of conscious and subconscious habits and behavior patterns that make us the special and unique persons we are.

Habits, then, are important in our overall development and growth as human beings. Without them, we would be guided entirely by our conscious actions with little time to think about anything else. The freedom we have to perform simple tasks like writing, tying our shoes, and eating with utensils is the direct result of our experiences and conditioning. These tasks are extremely difficult during growth and development, but are made simple by the shaping of our behavior patterns into habits. The problem occurs when we begin to acquire habits regardless of whether they're good or bad, positively or negatively reinforced. We react to every stimulus and start the conditioning process over again without thinking about the consequences and without trying to reverse the process before it becomes an ingrained behavior.

Chronic stress response, then, is the end result of a runaway conditioning process gone awry. And like any other bad habit, it too needs to be controlled through changes in our attitudes, behavior patterns, and lifestyles. Throughout the remainder of this book, I've tried to illustrate ways in which we can break our stress response habit by using the power of the conditioning process to our advantage. By conditioning ourselves to spontaneously relax, to relieve tension, to cope with conflict, and to eliminate anxiety, we'll gain freedom from stress and improve not only the "quantity" but more importantly the quality of our lives.

2

Stress Signs and Symptoms

The second step in relieving stress is to use stress management techniques to eliminate stress reactions. The first step is to recognize certain symptoms that tell us our body is being stressed. In most cases that's not so easy, especially if the symptoms don't occur at the same time as the stress that causes them. But regardless of how stress affects us individually, it always leaves an unmistakable pattern of stress → symptom → illness. The trick is to recognize the symptom quickly and link it to the stress that preceded it. Therefore, in order to manage or eliminate stress, we need to develop an ability and a system for identifying stressors so we can cope with our own individual stress events before they become serious illnesses.

In this chapter, we'll see how stress produces obvious markers which we can pick up and use as fingerprints to identify the events in our lives that cause stress. We'll also see how these symptoms can be produced and intensified by the kind of personality we have. Being able to recognize certain stress-producing traits in our personality can help us modify those traits in order to relieve stress symptoms.

Recognizing Stress Symptoms

Not every reaction we have is a symptom of stress. We need to remember that we're all different. What may be a stress signal for one individual may be a sign of disease for another, or even a normal response for someone else. But a common mistake many of us make is to blame stress symptoms or illnesses on things unrelated to stress. As a result, we miss the real warning signs of the stress response. Here are some typical examples:

Bill starts having stomach pains and occasional diarrhea when he goes to work. Instead of linking these symptoms with something happening at his job, he tries to figure out what it is he's been eating that's making him ill. By automatically assuming that stomach pain and diarrhea are caused by food, Bill's ignoring his body's cry for stress relief.

Joan begins to have back and neck pains during different parts of the day. She immediately thinks that her pains are caused by the way she has been sleeping at night or the way she has been sitting at her desk. By not realizing that her neck and back pains are caused by muscle tension during specific periods of stress, Joan is setting herself up for more frequent and more serious stress problems. Both Joan and Bill are typical victims of stress without knowing it because they haven't conditioned themselves to be aware of their body's stress signals.

Stress Symptom Checklist

Stress symptoms or signals can be divided into three main categories: physical, emotional, and behavioral symptoms. At the beginning of this book, I said that stress is the cause of more ailments and illnesses than anything known to modern medicine. Many of the symptoms listed below start out as minor irritants but become progressively worse and may lead to serious stress-related diseases. Although not exclusively limited to stress, following are many of the symptoms known to be associated with stress:

Physical Symptoms

- [ ] headaches (forehead or back of head)
- [ ] twitching eyelid
- [ ] twitching nose
- [ ] facial or jaw pains
- [ ] dry mouth or throat
- [ ] difficulty swallowing
- [ ] ulcers on tongue
- [ ] neck pains
- [ ] dizziness
- [ ] speech difficulties like slurring or stuttering
- [ ] backaches
- [ ] muscle aches
- [ ] weakness
- [ ] constipation
- [ ] indigestion
- [ ] nausea and/or vomiting
- [ ] stomach pains

- [ ] diarrhea
- [ ] gain or loss in weight
- [ ] loss of appetite or constant appetite
- [ ] rashes, hives, or other skin problems
- [ ] chest pains
- [ ] heartburn
- [ ] heart palpitations
- [ ] frequent urination
- [ ] cold hands and/or feet
- [ ] excessive sweating
- [ ] insomnia
- [ ] excessive sleeping
- [ ] sexual inadequacy
- [ ] high blood pressure
- [ ] chronic fatigue
- [ ] swollen joints
- [ ] increased allergies
- [ ] frequent colds or flu
- [ ] trembling and/or nervous tics
- [ ] accident proneness
- [ ] excessive menstruation or menstrual distress
- [ ] rapid or difficult breathing

Emotional Symptoms

- [ ] irritability
- [ ] moodiness
- [ ] depression
- [ ] unusual aggressiveness
- [ ] loss of memory or concentration
- [ ] restlessness or overexcitability
- [ ] nervousness about little things
- [ ] nightmares
- [ ] impulsive behavior
- [ ] feelings of helplessness or frustration
- [ ] withdrawal from other people
- [ ] neurotic behavior
- [ ] racing thoughts or disorientation
- [ ] anger
- [ ] inability to make decisions
- [ ] anxiety
- [ ] feelings of panic

☐ frequent episodes of crying
☐ thoughts of suicide
☐ feelings of losing control
☐ lack of interest in sex
☐ periods of confusion

Behavioral Symptoms

☐ gnashing or grinding teeth
☐ wrinkling forehead
☐ high-pitched nervous laughter
☐ foot or finger tapping
☐ nail biting
☐ hair pulling or twirling
☐ increased smoking
☐ increased use of prescribed medication
☐ increased alcohol consumption
☐ compulsive eating
☐ compulsive dieting
☐ pacing the floor
☐ chronic procrastination
☐ loss of interest in physical appearance
☐ sudden change in social habits
☐ chronic tardiness

Certain areas of the body and certain muscle groups are especially good indicators of stress reactions. Figures 2a and 2b illustrate those areas that are most frequently affected by stress. We need to be aware of any dull aches, sharp pains, nervous twitching, and sudden throbbing that occur in these areas during tense or stressful situations. Pain in these areas doesn't always indicate stress, but in the majority of cases, it's a sure bet that it does.

Most of us have no idea that stress can be the cause of so many different kinds of physical, emotional, and behavioral problems. When we think of stress, we automatically think of the usual symptoms like headaches, stomach pains, or muscle tensions. Other symptoms are attributed to things like diet, overexertion, weather, or normal muscle strains. The reason we don't recognize these minor stress symptoms is that we've become used to looking for the more common physical signals that we read about in health articles and newspapers. The thinking is, if there's no pain or illness involved, there's no stress problem to worry about. The truth is almost any

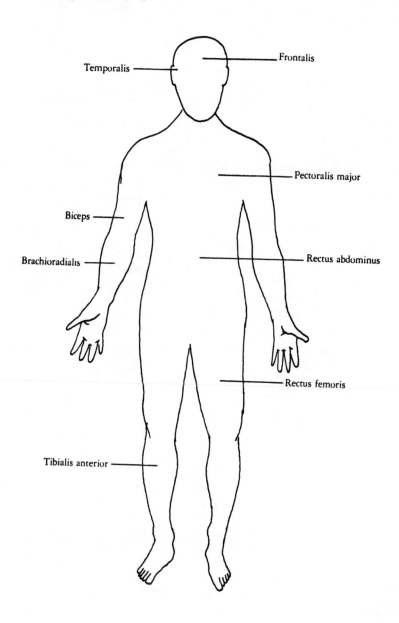

Figure 2a.
Major Muscle Groups affected by stress. Front side.

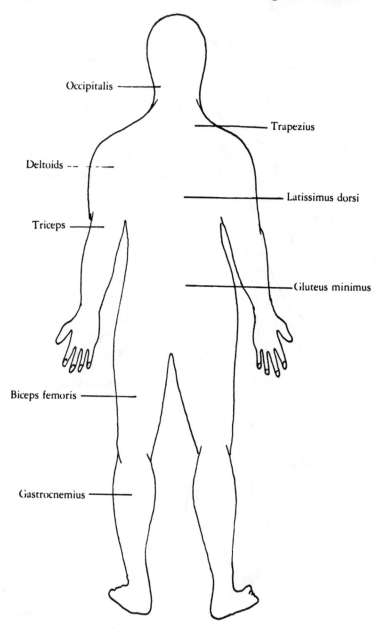

Figure 2b
Major muscle groups affected by stress. Back side.

kind of symptom can be a hidden signal of stress. Learning to recognize the small, insignificant signals can help us become more aware of our own sources of stress, prevent us from developing more serious symptoms, and make stress management a whole lot easier.

Linking Stress Symptoms to Stress Sources

One of the best ways to identify stress response patterns or hidden sources of stress is to keep a stress diary for at least two or three weeks. Unless we can clearly and systematically link symptoms to stress, we won't recognize the undetectable sources of stress that become a hidden part of our day-to-day routine. Once these hidden stressors get incorporated into our lives, they're much harder to identify because they're no longer obvious and unique. The only way to flush them out is to keep an accurate record of any events, feelings, emotions, and thoughts that lead to the symptoms they produce.

The following is a sample of what our stress diary might look like. It's divided into four separate columns for time of day, symptom, immediate activity, and previous activity. Entries are made as soon as a symptom is noticed so that nothing gets forgotten or omitted.

As soon as we notice a stress symptom (either one from the lists in this chapter or one of our own not listed), we should write it down right away along with the time of day or night it occurred, the activity we were doing or the thoughts we were having, and the activities and thoughts previous to the stress symptom. It's very important to include our thoughts as well as physical activities because thoughts can be even more potent triggers of stress symptoms than physical events.

And it's just as important to include previous activities and thoughts because stress reactions don't always occur at the same time that stress occurs. In many cases, symptoms involving physical pain or illness may not become noticeable for several hours following stress. Therefore, to get a true indication of what's really causing stress symptoms, we need to train ourselves to not only look at the present, but to look back and remember what we've experienced during the past several hours.

Day/Date_____

Time of day	Stress Symptom	Immediate Activity	Previous Activity
9:30 AM	Headache	Having breakfast Alone	Getting kids to school in a Rush (9:00 AM)
12:30 PM	muscle Pain in neck & shoulders	Watching T.V.	Thinking about paying bills.
6:00 Pm	Tapping foot constantly	Thinking about unpaid bills	Thinking about unpaid bills
10:00 Pm	Stomach pain	Argument with Daughter	Watching T.V.
12:00 PM	Insomnia	Feeling Anger About Argument	Feeling Anger About Argument

After a week of keeping a stress diary, start looking for patterns. Do you usually get symptoms at a certain time of day? Do you get a specific symptom every time you do a certain thing or think a certain thought? Do you get sick an hour or more after you do something?

This is when we begin to play detective and look for clues that will lead us to our own hidden sources of stress. For example, we may notice that at 9:30 AM almost every day, we get a terrible headache. On closer inspection, we see that at 9:00 AM each day, we were busy rushing the kids off to school. On Monday, Tuesday, and Friday, we had trouble falling asleep. Our diary tells us that on those nights, we thought a lot about problems at work. At 7:00 PM on Wednesday and Thursday, we had diarrhea. According to our stress diary, at 5:30 PM on those nights, we were worried about having to go to weekly staff meetings while leaving the kids home alone. Regardless of how insignificant our thoughts, feelings, or actions seem, we need to write them down. What might appear insignificant at the time could turn out to be a major trigger for stress symptoms.

Once we recognize our stress symptoms and link them to stress sources, the next step is to determine why the sources are causing the symptoms. We should ask ourselves these four questions:

1. Is the timing of the activity (time of day or night) causing stress symptoms?

2. Is the reason we're doing the activity causing stress symptoms?
3. Is the way we're doing the activity causing stress symptoms?
4. Is the amount of time spent doing the activity causing stress symptoms?

First, we need to assess whether or not it's the timing of whatever we're doing that's creating problems. Do the symptoms disappear when we change the time of activity? Is nighttime better than daytime? Does reorganizing our schedule make what we're doing less stressful? Next, we need to assess why we're doing what we're doing in the first place. Is it really necessary? Can we do without it? Next, we need to assess the manner in which we're doing what we're doing. Are we too intense? Do we worry the entire time? Do we use so much energy that we feel worn out? Finally, we need to assess how much time we spend doing what we're doing. Do we spend too much time? Do we spend too little time? Is the amount of time we spend interfering with more important things?

The answers to these questions tell us why the things we do, or the feelings we have, make us sick. Keeping an accurate stress diary will be physical proof that some of the little things we do, some of the little thoughts we have are not so little after all! They need to be changed if we're serious about managing our stress.

At the end of our stress diary, we need to write down three things: 1) the exact cause of our stress symptoms (a physical activity, a thought, etc.); 2) the reason why the activity is causing the symptoms (timing, the way we do it, the reason for doing it, etc.); and 3) our goals for eliminating the stress symptoms. We can write something like this:

1. Cause of headaches: rushing to get the kids off to school every morning.
2. Reason for symptoms: timing—not enough time to do everything—feel rushed.
3. Solution: a) get up a little earlier
     b) organize my morning hours more efficiently
     c) don't leave things till the last minute
     d) prepare the night before

We should check our stress diary each day so we're sure of meeting at least some of our goals. As we accomplish one goal, we need to move on to the next, and so on until we eliminate stress symptoms altogether. Eventually, our natural ability to recognize stress symptoms will become easier. We'll be able to identify stress sources instantly and act quickly before they become triggers for conditioned stress responses.

Even certain personality traits can be adjusted for our benefit if we recognize those traits as real sources of stress. "Type A" individuals, for example, are more prone to stress symptoms and stress reactions because they often don't link their symptoms with their normal behavior patterns. For them, keeping a stress diary is even more important than it is for the rest of us. But regardless of what type of personality type we are, we all need to realize that small and insignificant events can be major sources of stress and illness.

Recognizing "Type A" vs. "Type B" Behavior

When heart disease became our nation's number one killer, it was thought that anyone leading a stressful lifestyle was at risk. It's now well known that there's a certain behavior pattern called "Type A" which makes one more susceptible to coronary heart disease and other stress-related diseases because of specific character traits and mental attitudes. Many of these traits and attitudes are the reason for stress symptoms in the first place. Modifying Type A behavior patterns in order to relieve stress symptoms requires that we first detect the traits in ourselves that make us either Type A or Type B individuals. We can then use stress management techniques to gradually condition ourselves to alter those traits.

The following are some differences between Type A individuals and Type B individuals. Not all Type A's and Type B's will have all or even most of these traits, but people typically fall into one or the other category.

Type A Characteristics

> Intensely competitive
> Impatient
> Achievement oriented
> Aggressive and driven
> Having a distorted sense of time urgency
> Moving rapidly and frequently
> Talking fast and listening impatiently

Type B Characteristics

Relaxed and unhurried
Patient
Noncompetitive
Nonaggressive
Not having time urgency

In addition to these basic traits, Type A individuals have a greater cardiovascular response to stress, a greater increase in blood pressure, a greater release of adrenalin, higher blood cholesterol levels, and more extensive arteriosclerosis than Type B individuals. Type A individuals probably don't have all these problems at the same time, but they normally have enough of them to drastically increase their chances of becoming sick or diseased much sooner than Type B individuals.

Type A Behavior Quiz

Many times, stress symptoms are the direct result of Type A behavior. Unless we become aware of our own Type A traits, recognizing stress symptoms and linking them to stress sources can be very difficult. The following quiz is designed to give you an idea of your own behavioral type. Read each statement carefully and then circle the number corresponding to the category of behavior that best fits you. (1 = Never; 2 = Seldom; 3 = Sometimes; 4 = Usually; 5 = Always) When you finish, add up all the circled numbers. A key at the end of the quiz will explain what your total score means.

1. I become angry or irritated   1   2   3   4   5
    whenever I have to stand in line for more
    than 15 minutes.

2. I handle more than one problem   1   2   3   4   5
    at a time.

3. It's hard finding the time to relax   1   2   3   4   5
    and let myself go during the day.

4. I become irritated or annoyed   1   2   3   4   5
    when someone is speaking too slowly.

5. I try hard to win at sports or games.   1   2   3   4   5

6. When I lose at sports or games, I   1   2   3   4   5
    get angry at myself or others.

7. I have trouble doing special things   1   2   3   4   5
    for myself.

8. I work much better under pressure   1   2   3   4   5
    or when meeting deadlines.

9. I find myself looking at my watch   1   2   3   4   5
    whenever I'm sitting around or not
    doing something active.

10. I bring work home with me.   1   2   3   4   5

11. I feel energized and exhilarated   1   2   3   4   5
    after being in a pressure situation.

12. I feel like I need to take charge   1   2   3   4   5
    of a group in order to get things
    moving.

13. I find myself eating rapidly in   1   2   3   4   5
    order to get back to work.

14. I do things quickly regardless of   1   2   3   4   5
    whether I have time or not.

15. I interrupt what people are saying   1   2   3   4   5
    when I think they're wrong.

16. I'm inflexible and rigid when it   1   2   3   4   5
    comes to changes at work or at home.

17. I become jittery and need to move   1   2   3   4   5
    whenever I'm trying to relax.

18. I find myself eating faster than   1   2   3   4   5
    the people I'm eating with.

19. At work, I need to perform more   1 2 3 4 5
    than one task at a time in order to
    feel productive.

20. I take less vacation time than I'm   1 2 3 4 5
    entitled to.

21. I find myself being very picky and   1 2 3 4 5
    looking at small details.

22. I become annoyed at people who don't   1 2 3 4 5
    work as hard as I do.

23. I find that there aren't enough   1 2 3 4 5
    things to do during the day.

24. I spend a good deal of my time   1 2 3 4 5
    thinking about my work.

25. I get bored very easily.   1 2 3 4 5

26. I'm active on weekends either   1 2 3 4 5
    working or doing projects.

27. I get into arguments with people   1 2 3 4 5
    who don't think my way.

28. I have trouble "rolling with the   1 2 3 4 5
    punches" whenever problems arise.

29. I interrupt someone's conversation   1 2 3 4 5
    in order to speed things up.

30. I take everything I do seriously.   1 2 3 4 5

The minimum score is 30, the maximum 150. The breakdown by personality type is as follows:

Score	Personality Type
100–150	Type A
76–99	Type AB (Average)
30–75	Type B

If your score was 75 or below, you're a Type B person. You pretty much take life as it comes and usually don't allow problems and worries to dominate your life. If your score was in the range of 76 to 99, you're part of a majority who has some Type A and some Type B characteristics For the most part, you probably know how to relax and aren't very aggressive or competitive. You do, however, take some things seriously and, in certain situations, like to be active, competitive, and productive. You need to see which Type A traits you have and decide whether or not they're affecting your health and lifestyle. If your score was 100 or above, then chances are you're a Type A person and you need to work on your attitudes, behavior, and priorities before you become seriously ill.

Since every person is different, there really are no absolute right or wrong answers. What may be a traumatic experience for one person may be a cakewalk for someone else. But no one, regardless of how energized and excited stress makes them feel, can keep up with too many Type A behavior patterns and stay healthy for very long. In fact, it's well known that Type A's suffer from many more kinds of stress symptoms and get sick much more often than Type B's do.

Type B or Type AB behavior is good because it allows us to achieve goals, to be motivated and productive, and to do all the things Type A's can do without being hostile, aggressive, impatient, or insecure. Achieving everything we want while still maintaining our composure and being able to relax is something we can all learn to do. By modifying our Type A behavior patterns and conditioning ourselves to adopt more Type B character traits, we'll become sick less often and make our lives more enjoyable and stress free.

Modifying Type A Character Traits

We develop either Type A or Type B behavior as a result of our upbringing, our environment, and sometimes our genetic makeup. Therefore, modifying Type A behavior patterns in order to develop more Type B behavior patterns isn't achieved overnight. It takes practice and effort on our part and a sincere desire to want to change. But once we begin the process of adopting more Type B traits, it becomes easier and easier to conform because our brain will be trained to look at stressful situations in a completely different way. We'll see this more clearly in the next chapter when I discuss perceptions, conditioning, attitude changes, and behavior modification.

The key to modifying Type A behavior is to break some of the long-term stress habits we've acquired. We do this by practicing special exercises that force us to acquire new habits at the same time we get rid of old habits. Many of us have Type A traits, not because we're born with them, but because we've repeated Type A behavior patterns so often they've become an unnatural part of our real personality. In essence, we've picked up some bad Type A habits. By actually practicing Type B behavior exercises, we'll gradually condition ourselves to eliminate some of our worst and most obvious Type A behavior traits. Once that happens, we'll be able to confront stressful situations knowing we can use our new Type B habits to combat stress and prevent its symptoms.

Type B Behavior Exercises

The following are some practical exercises we can do to help us change our Type A habits and activities. After doing these kinds of exercises several times, we'll eventually be able to think up different exercises using our own particular Type A behavior patterns. Practicing these exercises is important in habit formation because the physical act of doing them is a much more powerful conditioner than just thinking about them. Conditioning, whether it's physical or mental, requires the combined efforts of our brain and our body in order to achieve positive and lasting effects.

- Determine what activities bring out Type A behavior and then reenact those activities using Type B behavior. For example, if standing in line triggers stress symptoms, the next time you have to stand in a long line, try to consciously practice not getting irritated or annoyed. Think about what you're going to do when you get home, about how nice the weekend is going to be on the golf course, about a funny thing you saw on television. Instead of thinking about being stuck in line, think about pleasant and relaxing things. Pretty soon, this kind of thinking will come easily and naturally.

- At meal time, put your knife and fork down between bites. This will force you to slow down your eating behavior and leave more room for conversation and interaction. Slowing down your eating habits will spill over into other activities and help you slow them down as well.

- Force yourself to do more recreational activities. Instead of reading job-related magazines or books, for example, buy a recreational book and enjoy it purely for the sake of reading pleasure. Make a date with yourself to go to a fun movie, take a joy ride in the country, or walk in the woods. Making yourself feel special will help you be more aware of any negative behaviors affecting your health.

- Spend an entire day without your watch. Clock watching and a sense of time urgency are major components of Type A behavior. Make a real effort to forget time and just enjoy the day without feeling rushed. At first, you'll be surprised at how often you look at your wrist. But when you finally realize that time isn't an important part of that day, you'll settle back and relax more. A few times without your watch will make you more aware of how nice it really is not to be a clock watcher.

- Turn every frown and negative facial expression into a smile. Every time you notice yourself tensing up your jaw, wrinkling your forehead, grimacing, or making any kind of unpleasant facial expression, immediately smile and keep smiling for at least one minute. This exercise will train you to become accutely aware of the difference between negative and positive expressions because the negative expressions will feel different and unpleasant. After a week or two of doing this exercise, any negative facial expression will instantly trigger a reaction to smile in order to relieve facial tension. Being aware of negative expressions will also allow you to recognize and link the source of those expressions more easily.

- Give yourself positive Type B self-instructions. Use expressions like relax, slow down, stay calm, don't rush, easy does it, etc. Verbalizing Type B behavior traits enhances the conditioning process and makes practicing more effective. Don't be afraid to verbalize out loud. Hearing your Type B self-instructions will add to their effectiveness because your brain will be getting the message in a loud and clear way. Eventually, Type B self-instructions will become so automatic that you'll be able to retrieve them from your subconscious without having to verbalize at all.

● Reward yourself for a whole week of Type B behavior. Choose a Type B behavior pattern (eating slowly, reading for pure enjoyment, waiting patiently in a long line, etc.) and follow it through for an entire week. At the end of a successful week, reward yourself with something special. Recognizing your accomplishment with a reward makes the conditioning process stronger and will go a long way toward changing the exercise from a practice session into routine behavior.

At the end of our stress diary, we should have a section set aside for writing down our Type A character traits, our goals for modifying them into Type B character traits, and whether or not any of our stress symptoms are eliminated as a result of our changing from Type A to Type B. Here's how it might look:

Type A Traits	Type A Stress Symptoms	Goals for Modifying Type A Behavior	Symptoms Eliminated?
Impatient About waiting	1. Grinding teeth 2. Neck pains	Think positive & pleasant Thoughts when waiting in a line	1. YES 2. YES
Overscheduling work. Trying To do too much.	1. Headaches	Schedule only 1 thing at a time. Take periodic breaks.	1. YES
Always in a Rush to go Somewhere	1. Stomach pains 2. General muscle tension	Get up earlier. Do advance planning. Organize time better	1. NO 2. YES

The idea behind practicing Type B character traits and keeping stress diary records is that once we recognize stress symptoms, become more aware of our behavior, and repeatedly perform constructive activities to modify that behavior, Type A stress management becomes a spontaneous one-minute mental exercise. That is, we eventually teach ourselves to "turn off" Type A character traits and "turn on" Type B character traits in as little as one minute because our brain will be conditioned to guide our behavior in a Type B way. Again, this doesn't come easily at first. We've spent a lifetime acquiring Type A habits. But if we use the simple principle of habit formation by physically doing Type B activities, we can gradually eliminate almost any Type A habit. Having done this, we'll not only become healthier and happier, but we'll feel better about ourselves for having the strength to change our habits and for finally bringing out the Type B person that has been inside us all along.

3

Good vs. Bad Stress

The stress response is basically the same in all of us. The degree to which it affects us depends entirely on how we handle stress to begin with. In the first chapter, we saw how conditioning shapes our behavior and forces us to develop habits that can bring on spontaneous and harmful stress reactions. These reactions slowly mount up and ultimately give rise to the illnesses and diseases we develop during the course of our lives. In this chapter, we'll see how stress can be either good or bad depending on how we perceive it, and how we can become "stress tolerant" by changing our attitudes and conditioning ourselves to look at stress in a new way.

The same conditioning process used to bring about stress reactions can be used to change our response to stress from one that's negative and harmful to one that's positive and beneficial. Getting into the habit of viewing stress as something constructive rather than destructive is the first step in our journey to becoming a more healthy and stress free person.

Stress Tolerance

We sometimes hear people say "I work better under pressure," or "I thrive on competition." These individuals perform much better when they're under the gun. They seem to be more satisfied when they're meeting deadlines, rushing to make sales, or doing anything else that enhances the excitement of their lives. They're members of a minority for whom stress isn't necessarily harmful and may actually be part and parcel of a very healthy and productive life. Occupations like physician, emergency room nurse, and air traffic controller tend to attract the kinds of people who are called "stress tolerant" and who probably wouldn't be completely happy without a daily dose of stress. For them, stress tolerance is the end result of a conditioning process that automatically takes negative situations and transforms them into positive events.

We too can develop the kind of stress tolerance these people have without changing our personalities and without having to be pressured all the time in order to feel good. The way in which we perceive and interpret events and situations is what makes us either tolerant of or prone to the effects of stress reactions. Learning to do this is one of the most critical elements in stress management.

In general, we can say that good stress results from situations we can control. Bad stress results from situations over which we have no control. One of the most popular theories about stress suggests that stress tolerant individuals possess a certain attitude toward life that includes having a sense of control over events, having commitment and a sense of purpose, being open to change, and viewing change as a challenge rather than a threat. Stress prone individuals, on the other hand, are overwhelmed because they feel powerless to control or influence the events around them.

For stress tolerant individuals, the ideal is not to avoid stress, but to become involved in stress situations in order to overcome obstacles and meet challenges. The transition from stress proneness to stress tolerance is achieved through learning, conditioning, habit formation, and the ability to see something positive in every stressful encounter. All these things are accomplished by changing our thought patterns and by reconditioning ourselves to interpret stressful events in a way that will make them work to our advantage.

One of the most important factors that determines to what extent stress affects us is how we perceive the impact of that stress on our lives. Stress perception is influenced by age, intelligence, income, level of education, religion, previous experiences, and personality type. For example, if we're expected to solve a difficult problem, we're naturally less stressed if we have the education and intelligence to solve the problem than if we don't. This is a real source of job stress for people put into positions they can't handle or placed in jobs for which they're not qualified. Likewise, if we're wealthy, our job security isn't as stressful as it would be if we needed the job in order to support a large family. In essence, the way we perceive how stress is going to affect us personally is the critical factor in our subconscious decision of how we ultimately deal with stress at any given time.

Perceptions Are Either Positive or Negative

The first and most important mental reaction that occurs whenever we encounter any kind of situation or event is our perception of that event as either positive or negative. Figure 3a illustrates how

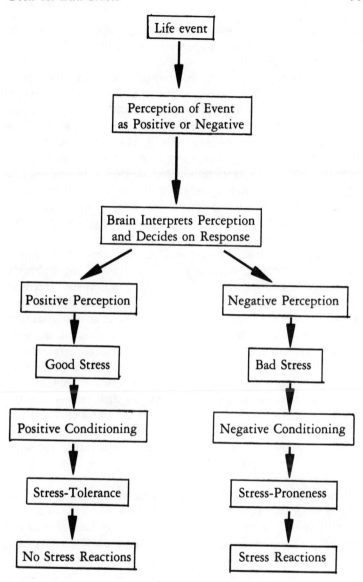

Figure 3a
Mental pathway through which
life events become stress responses

our brain receives information, perceives it as either positive or negative, interprets it, decides how to respond, and conditions us to form habits leading to stress tolerance or stress proneness. Based only on our perception, we immediately interpret an event and make instant decisions about how to respond to it. If we perceive the event as no threat, we either respond in a positive way or we don't respond at all. If, on the other hand, we interpret the event as a threat, we respond with negative stress reactions. By altering our perceptions, we slowly change the conditioning process because we begin to interpret events with new meaning. Perception of events, then, is very important in stress management because it's the beginning element from which all our decisions concerning stress are made. Let's look at some specific examples of how the perception of life events determines stress tolerance.

A study done with nurses showed that nonintensive care nurses experienced much higher levels of anxiety, reported more physical ailments, and had greater work load dissatisfaction than intensive care nurses did. It was later found that the intensive care nurses wanted (or needed) more challenge and felt more adventurous than nonintensive care nurses. These two factors enabled the intensive care nurses to perceive stress differently than their counterparts and, therefore, they were able to minimize job-related anxiety and stress.

In a study done with business executives, it was discovered that the executives who remained healthy during their careers were the ones who had a sense of commitment, felt in control of their lives, and sought novelty and change rather than familiarity and security. They viewed change as an opportunity and a challenge, and when stress did occur, they became enthusiastic and energized instead of worried and depressed.

When a group of lawyers was studied, it was found that the lawyers who were seen as least stressed were often the ones who became physically sick the most often—exactly opposite of what was expected! After looking more closely at how lawyers are trained during their four years of law school, it became clear why this happens. Lawyers are conditioned to believe they perform best under pressure. Thus, their perception of stress allows them to deal with it in a nonthreatening and even beneficial way. Their conditioning makes them believe that stress brings out the best in them and, therefore, they respond to stress in just the opposite way from most of us.

All three of these studies demonstrate that certain individuals respond to stress in a positive way only because they're able to perceive stress events as challenging, rewarding experiences. In many cases, becoming stress tolerant happens early during our development and remains with us as a positive habit throughout life. But even if it doesn't, we can still have control over how we respond to stress by using the power of our brain to change our perceptions and guide our attitudes. Once we do that, we can overcome our own natural tendencies to be stress prone and join the ranks of the stress tolerant.

Stress Tolerant or Stress Prone
Which Are You?

There are basically three types of individual: the type who can't get along well without a stressful lifestyle; the type who can't get along well without a quiet, peaceful life; and the type who has the ability to get along perfectly with or without stress. A certain amount of stress is essential for normal health, as long as the amount doesn't exceed the coping ability of our own personality. The danger comes when we mismatch our personality type and try to become something we're not. When that happens, our normal personality becomes inhibited and we either get too much or too little stress (usually too much).

Unfortunately, stress tolerance can be very deceptive, and many individuals in high-stress careers make the mistake of thinking that they as a group are stress tolerant. Careers don't make people stress tolerant. If that were true, there wouldn't be so many heart attack and ulcer victims among executives, doctors, air traffic controllers, and others in high-stress occupations. These individuals try to be stress tolerant without first developing a proper attitude or without using stress management techniques to help them boost their stress tolerance. Thinking we're stress tolerant, regardless of occupation, is a deadly mistake, especially if we've been subconsciously conditioned to be stress prone all along.

Knowing which personality type we are is important in deciding the kind of lifestyle we choose and the kinds of activities we need to avoid. Before we can work toward becoming stress tolerant, however, we need to examine the type of personality we have in order to make the transition from stress proneness to stress tolerance easier.

In the previous chapter, I described how to recognize stress symptoms and how to determine whether we're Type A or Type B individuals. Recognizing stress proneness is based on the same principle and the same technique. If, for example, we're sitting at home with nothing to do but read or watch television and we notice ourselves getting jumpy and irritable, we may be the kind of person who needs a stress stimulus. If we feel absolutely energized and exhilarated after being in a stressful situation, we may be one of a few who thrive on stress. If we notice that we get stomach pains, headaches, or backaches and become nervous and anxious whenever we're stressed, we know we're definitely not stress tolerant and shouldn't be pushing ourselves into pressure situations unless we learn to develop stress tolerant attitudes.

Unfortunately, most of us don't have the luxury of choosing what our day-to-day experiences will be like. We go to work and are forced to confront situations that lead to stress, anxiety, and depression. Some of us feel helpless and alienated because we can't or won't take control over the events in our lives. These feelings intensify and eventually grow into major emotional problems leading to ulcers, heart attacks, hypertension, and many other stress-related illnesses. In order to prevent this from happening, we need to develop a specific attitude called a "stress-plus" or "stress tolerant" attitude. This kind of attitude changes the way our brain interprets events and conditions us to automatically or habitually turn negative situations into positive experiences.

Developing a Stress Tolerant Attitude

Stress tolerance begins in our brain. More specifically, it begins at the very moment our brain picks up a stress signal and perceives it a certain way. This is the stage of habit formation we must attack and change in order to begin the conditioning process needed to become stress tolerant. During this stage, there are five mental images or thought patterns that have to be present for stress to work for us instead of against us. These mental images need to become part of our conscious day-to-day existence so that they're incorporated into our routine behavior patterns and become ingrained as habits. Once they're part of our normal thought processes, these images also become spontaneous and, acting together, end up being a natural and positive response to any kind of stress event.

The following is a list, along with descriptions, of the five mental images necessary for developing stress tolerance. Read and reread them slowly and as often as it takes until they're completely familiar. More importantly, put them into practice every chance you get so you can begin to recondition yourself to perceive and interpret life events as sources of "good stress."

Mental Image #1. *I get a feeling of accomplishment and strength whenever I'm committed or involved.*

Whenever we become committed to a project, activity, or job, we develop a sense of worth that's important in how we feel about ourselves and what we're doing. Becoming actively involved and committed gives us purpose and direction. We begin to lose the negative attitudes that stress brings on. Most of us tend to be passive rather than active. By actively participating and being involved and committed, we'll have a better outlook on life and feel much better about ourselves in general. When that happens, we'll automatically begin to experience more positive and less negative events.

Mental Image #2. *I find change and/or challenge an exciting and rewarding experience.*

Too often we view changes in our lives as negative experiences. Even more often, we allow changes to occur without making any effort at all to make positive experiences out of them. And sometimes, we view change as neither positive nor negative and develop an attitude of complacency which causes us to have little if any feeling of excitement about anything. We should always be prepared to visualize the plus side of change rather than dwell on the minus side. Get in the habit of thinking about any change or challenge as exciting and rewarding. The more we do this, the less negatively we'll feel and the more excited we'll get.

A simple trick to use whenever we find that changing our routine is causing some anxiety is to do something special for ourselves at the start of each day. For example, we can begin the day by taking a walk, having a cup of tea and reading the paper, or sitting quietly and listening to our favorite program on the radio. Doing a little something extra for ourselves will make us feel special and give us the incentive to go out and meet those changes and challenges head on.

Mental Image #3. *I get a feeling of power that energizes me whenever I take control of situations.*

Having a feeling of control over events and situations is probably the most important and fundamental attitude we need in order to turn bad stress into good stress. We're discovering that bad stress isn't a result of job pressures and negative events but rather of the feelings we have that what we do is useless and that life is too complex and beyond our personal control. There's absolutely no way that we can receive any kind of positive feedback from a stress situation unless we feel like we have some kind of control over that situation. And if we feel in control, we have no problem channeling our energy into constructive activities.

One of the biggest problems we face as stress prone individuals is our inability to be in control of events that we should have been in control over all along. The more we begin to lose control, the more negatively we begin to feel and the more stressed we become. Eventually, every situation we encounter is one that we have little or no control over at all.

Having control is actually related to being involved and committed because involvement and commitment give us a sense of control and allow us to develop behavior patterns that automatically put us in control. Once we begin to feel like we're in charge of situations, we'll start meeting them head on instead of worrying about how they'll affect us. Soon, we'll realize that controlling is much easier and more rewarding for us than always being controlled.

Mental Image #4. *Stress brings out the qualities in me that make me most productive and worthwhile.*

Why would we willingly want to think that anything has the power to make us worthless and unproductive? Why should we deny ourselves the opportunity to be a better person just because we happen to be under pressure or stress? Imagine stress to be a battery that energizes us and without which we wouldn't be able to reach our full potential.

Good athletes know that, in order to perform well, they need intense competition and pressure. The great ones have developed the attitude that unless they're under pressure, they're just not going to be at their peak. This is why most world sporting records are set during the Olympics or during competitions when the best athletes are competing. These athletes actually believe that only the stress of competition brings out their best qualities. Their bodies respond to what their brain has been conditioned to perceive and, therefore, they need that extra pressure to stimulate themselves into making stress work for them. We need to become athletes in the sense that our performance and attitude will always be better when we're challenged. We'll quickly discover how effective stress can be in giving us the incentive to do our very best.

Mental Image #5. *I can transform any stressful situation into something positive.*

There's absolutely no reason why we can't think of something positive that will result from most stressful situations. When we can finally put this idea into practice, we'll have overcome the biggest obstacle in our becoming stress tolerant! The idea that we should be able to transform something negative into something positive is, in a way, a culmination of the first four mental attitudes. That is, if we become involved and committed, we'll begin to have a feeling of control over situations and make those situations exciting and rewarding experiences. Once that happens, we'll subconsciously and automatically believe that those same situations bring out the best in us and make us more productive and worthwhile. All these factors will naturally make us feel we can turn just about any negative event into a positive experience.

Integrating all these mental images into our own personality conditions us to make a conscientious effort to adopt a more positive attitude about stress. The attitude we choose determines whether or not we allow events to control us or whether we control them. And, consequently, whether or not we perceive stress as a challenge that we can overcome and mold to our own benefit. This small adjustment in the way we view challenges is the basic principle behind stress tolerance. By incorporating this simple principle into our daily lives, we can turn stress into a driving force that will enable us to perceive negative events in a very positive and constructive way.

Attitude vs. Personality:
Changing One Without the Other

Our attitudes are the mental processes we use to respond to stimuli. Our personality is the sum total of years of habitual physical and mental activities, attitudes, interests, and behaviors. It's who we are and what makes us different from anyone else. Because personality is such a strong human trait, we tend to think that everything we do, every emotion we possess, is the end result of our personality. We give up on change and improvement in our lives because we make the mistake of believing that somehow our attitudes and behaviors are an inseparable part of our personality. As a result, we deny ourselves the opportunity to try new things and become better human beings.

For some of us, it seems impossible to turn bad situations into good ones and even more impossible to transform those bad situations into rewarding and exhilarating experiences no matter how much we try. The solution is not to try and change our basic personality type in order to meet challenges, but rather to change our way of coping and handling stressful situations through techniques that change our basic attitudes.

Because our personality is molded during the first few years of life, it's a serious mistake to try and cope with stress through total personality change. At work, for example, we shouldn't alter our basic personality to one that a chief executive officer at a major corporation would have. That executive officer is there because, most likely, his or her personality fits that position and has been shaped by certain environmental factors and upbringing. Executives who try to fit into that kind of mold without having the personality for it are the ones who become sick most often. Here's an example:

Jim is naturally a shy and nonaggressive person. When he gets promoted to an executive position, he takes on more responsibilities and a tougher workload. Instead of changing his attitude about work and trying to cope with his new job by adjusting some of his work habits, he becomes more aggressive and demanding because he feels like that's what it takes to get the job done. Because Jim's new personality type is not really Jim, he soon develops stress-related problems. Jim didn't realize that a simple change in his attitude and some changes in his behavior patterns would have been more effective than changing his basic personality type. Trying to change our personality can do a lot of damage to our physical and mental health. Our body will always recognize an abnormal change in our personality and respond negatively even though we may consciously think that we've handled stress in a positive way.

People like Jim need to learn that coping with stress by changing our attitudes is different than changing our basic personality. We have to know our personality and recognize its capacity for stress; we have to exist within the limits of our own personality. At the same time, we must realize that some of our attitudes don't necessarily have to be rigid and uncompromising. The real key to meeting stressful challenges in a positive way is not to alter our identity but to alter our attitudes so that we can cope with stress within the limits of our own self.

But even with a change of attitude, we should never lose sight of the fact that we can't subject ourselves to daily, long-term stress and expect to remain healthy for very long without using stress management techniques and exercises to diminish the effects. Regardless of how much challenge or pressure we think we may need to perform our best, for many of us, the stress response will remain a real and constant threat. Even if we successfully develop stress tolerant attitudes, unless we learn to eliminate that threat through behavior changes, relaxation techniques, and coping strategies, the stress response will slowly and unexpectedly manifest itself as one of many stress-related illnesses or diseases. The relaxation techniques discussed in later chapters will help us add to our stress tolerance by giving us the tools we need to cope.

Turning Bad Stress Into Good Through Behavior Modification

One of the ways we fight stress is to change our attitudes in order to perceive negative events in a positive way. Another way is to modify some of our behavior patterns so it becomes easier for us to change those attitudes and make them fit our own personality. Our attitudes and our behavior are closely linked; behavior can control our attitudes and attitudes can certainly drive our behavior. Changing some of our behavior patterns is critical to stress management and can make the difference between our being able to develop stress tolerance or not. Here are some simple behavior changes we can adopt which should make our attitude changes much easier.

- Talk to yourself in a positive way. Whenever we find ourselves in a stressful situation, the worst thing we can do is say something negative to ourselves. If we're waiting in a line for a long time, for example, rather than complain and get irritable, we should say something positive to ourselves that will relieve tension and help us relax.

- Visualize positive, not negative stress results. One of the most common things we do when we expect to be stressed is "spectatoring" or visualizing what's going to happen to us. Most sexual problems, for example, are aggravated or caused by spectatoring. Another term for this is "performance anxiety," where we look at ourselves through someone else's eyes. We become nervous or anxious whenever we begin to think about how we're going to perform a certain task. Instead of imagining failure, imagine success. Once we get used to thinking about good results—expecting success—thinking positively about the outcome of stressful situations will come naturally.

- Be flexible enough to change. Regardless of our ability to cope with stress, we need to realize that everyone is different when it comes to doing things. What works for some individuals may not work for others. We shouldn't hesitate to change the way we approach problems. By being flexible, we may find a better method of accomplishing our goals and organizing our lives.

Rather than thinking of change as a weakness, we should think of it as a strength because we have the wisdom and courage to try and do things a better way.

● Never try to be perfect. Although we should always strive to improve, we should accept ourselves for what we are. Perfection doesn't exist in anyone. Instead of constantly telling ourselves what we should be like, we should be telling ourselves that we're the best we could be.

● Take time out. We need to treat ourselves to periodic breaks for rest, exercise, hobbies, and socializing. It's well known that few of us can work for more than two or three hours without losing our ability to concentrate. We need to take a ten or fifteen minute break every few hours just to set our minds free and get back into a good frame of mind. We should also schedule some time to go out for lunch or go to dinner and a show. Taking time out to do things for ourselves makes us feel we're important and that we care about ourselves. When we make ourselves feel special, we automatically have a much better outlook on life and improve our capacity to change even the worst of our attitudes.

● Find the best work time and environment. Everyone has a time of day or night when they feel most efficient and/or relaxed. Most of us are either morning people or night people. We should determine our best time and plan as much of our schedule as possible around that time, doing our most difficult work at our peak energy levels. We should also think about small things like what kind of music makes us most relaxed, what kinds of pictures we enjoy looking at, and what color scheme soothes us.

● Use exercise as a stress reliever. Exercise is one of the best ways to relieve tension and anxiety. It not only makes us feel more energized and invigorated, it also gives our immune system a boost to help us fight off illness during stress reactions. Exercise also helps us relax by releasing the body's natural tranquilizer—endorphin. Endorphin not only suppresses pain, but acts to give us a feeling of well-being and euphoria. The natural high we get from endorphin is a good countermeasure to the tension and anxiety we experience from stress and helps us become more receptive to attitude and behavior changes.

- Don't dwell on the past. Thinking about what we should have done or said makes us have doubts about ourselves. We can't do anything about the past, just the present, and perhaps the future. Instead of worrying about what happened, we should use past experiences in a positive way saying to ourselves, "Okay, I didn't want to do it that way. I'll do it this way next time." After we say that, we should forget about it and go on to more important things.

- If everything else fails, change or avoid the situation. There's going to come a time when we encounter a situation that we just can't handle regardless of how much we try. All of us have traits in our personality that simply won't allow us to cope with certain situations even if we change our attitudes and behavior. When that happens, there's nothing left to do but change or avoid the situation altogether. This may be hard to do, especially if the situation is a job or a career. In that case, a difficult choice has to be made between the possible long-term physical and emotional effects of stress and the importance of keeping the job or career. Most people, however, find that using all the stress management techniques available, including attitude and behavior modification and relaxation training, helps them improve their situations to the point of being able to cope with the most adverse conditions.

Turning negative events into positive experiences requires that we make adjustments in the way we think and in the way we act. Regardless of the kind of personality we have, conditioning ourselves to cope with stress through changes in our attitudes and behavior is the key element in developing a stress tolerant lifestyle.

All of us fall into certain personality molds that give us character and make us unique individuals with different interests and varying behavior patterns. Somewhere within all of us, however, lies the ability to bring out the best in ourselves. We have the power to turn bad stress into good. How we perceive life events, how we behave in response to stress encounters, and how we condition ourselves to look at negative situations in a positive way all determine how quickly and easily we can begin to break the stress habit.

4

Job Stress And Burnout

The attitude that work is a duty and an obligation is deeply rooted in our culture. It began with the early pioneers who settled this land and who believed that success and survival could only be achieved through cooperation, determination, and hard labor. This positive attitude toward work continued from generation to generation until America suddenly began to evolve into a new and totally different society—one that no longer placed as high a value on shared responsibility and mutual coexistence. And as our society evolved, so did our concept of work. Instead of asking the question "how will my work affect my community and my neighbors," we began to ask "how will I be affected by what I do?"

The idea of using work as a means of improving society was gradually replaced by the idea of using work to enhance our own status and standard of living. It's when this attitude crept into our normal way of thinking that work became yet another source of stress. It now ranks as one of the leading causes of physical and emotional disorders and affects nearly every aspect of our society in terms of health care costs, insurance rates, absenteeism, economic problems, and national productivity. Because job stress is becoming such a routine part of our daily lives, relieving stress through changes in work habits, work environment, and worker relations must be a key element in our overall stress management strategy. In this chapter, I'll discuss various ways to improve our work-related attitudes and behaviors so that job stress, if not totally eliminated, can at least be kept under manageable control.

Sources of Job Stress

Just about any work situation we're involved in can be a potential source of stress. The way in which we perceive those work situations will determine to what extent we're stressed and whether or not we'll experience serious stress symptoms. As we learned in chapter 3, our response to stress (in this case, job stress) is either negative or positive depending on how we elect to perceive and interpret that stress and how we ultimately choose to deal with it.

In order to manage job stress more effectively, we must first be able to recognize the things about our work that are causing pressure. With few exceptions, the most common factors having the biggest negative impact on our health and job performance are emotionally-related stressors. Sometimes we don't think of emotional problems as sources of stress and, consequently, we don't do anything about them. More frequently though, we recognize emotional stress sources but don't do anything about them because we feel like we have no control over them. But changing even a small part of these stress factors can have a big effect on how we do our jobs and how we feel about going to work each day. In many cases, a very small change in the way we manage our time or in the way we set our priorities can make us feel so good that other stress sources seem insignificant and not worth getting sick over.

Following are ten of the most common job-related stress factors. All of us have our own stress factors besides those listed below. Recognizing the ones that affect us personally is an important first step in beginning our stress management strategy.

Common Job Stress Factors

- Not being organized or able to manage time effectively
- Having conflicts with supervisors, workers, or colleagues
- Not being able or qualified to do the job
- Feeling overwhelmed or overburdened by work
- Having too much or too little responsibility
- Not being able to meet deadlines
- Not being able to adapt to changes in work routine
- Not being able to utilize our skills and abilities
- Feeling that work is boring and meaningless
- Not getting any support from supervisors and managers

For the of us who find ourselves in situations where we can't make changes or decisions that will eliminate specific job stress factors, the best we can do is practice attitude and behavior modification exercises discussed in this and previous chapters. We should also take time to learn relaxation techniques and time management strategies described in later chapters.

The first step, however, is to identify and write down anything about our work that leads to stress symptoms. We should do this in exactly the same way we do our daily stress diary except that, in this case, we write down specific stress relief goals related to our job. Thinking of job stress as just another kind of strain that needs to be controlled through conditioning and habit formation makes stress management much easier than if we give job stress a special label of its own. Remember, no matter what the stress, recognizing the symptoms, identifying the sources, and setting specific goals to eliminate or relieve the sources are the three most important steps in successful stress management.

Supervisors and managers can also do a great deal to eliminate stress factors at work by following a few simple but important guidelines that can turn troubled workers into happy, productive employees. There's an added benefit. Many times, managers experience even more stress than workers as a direct result of negative and hostile feelings brought on by job stress factors. Therefore, everyone has a stake in creating a more stress free workplace. Managers and supervisors have a bigger stake because they not only feel the brunt of stress from one worker, but from every worker who recognizes them as the major source of his or her stress symptoms. The next section contains some practical changes that managers can make to help relieve job stress for everyone, including themselves.

Management's Role in Eliminating Job Stress

Managers have a special obligation to be aware of basic worker needs that have to be filled in order to ensure job satisfaction and prevent chronic job stress. According to a worker survey, taken by the U.S. Department of Commerce, there are certain things workers prefer most often in a job and things they don't consider as important if their other needs are met. A list, along with a question, was given to workers who were asked to choose, in order of importance, the things they wanted most out of work. Here are the results.

List of Job Factors

Security:	No danger of being fired
Income:	High wages
Meaning:	Work is important and gives a feeling of accomplishment
Hours:	Working hours are short; there's a lot of free time
Promotions:	Chances for advancement

Question: Which "one" thing on the above list do you
                     "most" prefer in a job? Which comes next? Which
                     comes third? etc.

Results: Most Important: Meaning
                     Second in Importance: Promotion
                     Third in Importance: Income
                     Fourth in Importance: Security
                     Fifth in Importance: Hours

The strongest expectations workers had were that their work be meaningful and that they have an opportunity to be promoted and compensated for their efforts. It didn't seem to matter as much to workers how much free time they got or how many hours they had to work. If they had a feeling of accomplishment in their work and were recognized for it, their job satisfaction was high and their job stress was almost nonexistent. The simple truth is, we all have a need to be worthwhile, and we all have a need to be rewarded for the good things we do. Successful managers and successful companies are in tune with these basic human desires and try to create a work environment that encompasses both.

Creating a Stress Free Work Environment

Besides basic job needs, managers also need to be aware of other job stress factors such as management style, utilizing workers' abilities, improving work conditions etc. Anything managers do that enhances positive attitudes and feelings or improves the way workers perceive their work will go a long way toward creating a stress free workplace. Here are nine sure-fire methods that will do just that.

1.   Develop better worker-manager relationships. Many under-
     lying causes of stress can be traced directly to personality
     differences between managers and workers. More and more
     companies are looking at management style as a criteria for
     promoting individuals to executive positions because job
     satisfaction and productivity are often linked to how well
     employees are handled. According to a recent study, top
     corporations are keenly aware of management personality
     flaws that are a source of severe job stress. The four most
     common flaws leading to stress and responsible for a
     manager's ultimate downfall are:

    a.   Insensitivity to others; having an abrasive, abusive, and intimidating management style.

    b.   Cold, aloof, and arrogant.

    c.   Overly ambitious; playing politics and using others to get promoted.

    d.   Overdemanding and unfair.

Taking a good look at management style and then improving or changing that style can help eliminate job stress for both manager and worker.

2. Utilize employee skills, potential, education, and abilities. Most of us need to be utilized to our full potential in order to be satisfied. Boredom, job dissatisfaction, anger, and hostility can be eliminated by finding out what employees are capable of doing and then increasing their responsibilities accordingly. Added responsibility makes employees feel needed and important—two vital ingredients necessary for company loyalty and job satisfaction.

    Employees can also be involved in decision making, even if it's on a small scale. Companies that initiate programs which include lower-level workers in the decision-making process find that their workers begin to take more initiative and responsibilities because they feel like they're an integral part of the total work effort. And once workers begin to take on more responsibilities, managers become less stressed because they have more time for their own responsibilities and don't feel as burdened or overworked.

3. Improve working conditions. Working conditions may include long hours, shift work, work overloads, poor surroundings, etc. Being insensitive to these conditions causes worker alienation, resentment, and job dissatisfaction. Since job conditions themselves often reflect a company's attitudes, workers begin to identify those conditions with the company and eventually become bad employees. Ultimately, bad working conditions lead to negative mental attitudes which are manifested as illness, absenteeism, and disease. When these things begin to affect the manager's job performance, he or she becomes stressed and takes it out on his or her workers. This vicious cycle can be eliminated if managers make an effort to create a work environment that's pleasant and enjoyable.

4. Give positive feedback. Everyone needs to know how they're doing. Feedback from managers gives workers the opportunity to correct mistakes and improve job skills. Likewise, positive feedback lets workers know they're appreciated and reassures them that they're performing well. Feedback (either to correct mistakes or to recognize good work) is important in letting workers know that what they do matters to the company.

5. Become a source of support—not supervision. All managers should learn the art of management by diplomacy. Very often, managers develop abrasive and insensitive styles that turn workers off and cause resentment and hostility. Instead of coming to a manager for advice and support, workers begin to avoid the manager altogether. Eventually, worker and manager become isolated, lines of communication are broken, and the work environment becomes very tense and unpleasant. In order to maintain a stress free work relationship, managers must recognize the importance of leadership and diplomacy. Without them, there can never be respect and loyalty.

6. Adopt fair promotional practices. One of the biggest reasons for job stress and job dissatisfaction is being unjustly passed over for promotion or advancement. The issue of fairness in promotion is very important in terms of how workers perceive a company's interest and concern for them as individuals and as valuable members of the company team.

7. Identify and recognize achievement. All of us, regardless of age, sex, or personality, need to be complimented and recognized occasionally for a job well done. There's nothing more demoralizing or frustrating than going out of one's way to do good work only to be ignored or told that good work is expected anyway. A kind or encouraging word of praise is worth its weight in gold for job satisfaction and good job performance. A stress free workplace goes hand in hand with praise, recognition, fairness, and a positive management style.

8. Avoid putting workers in role conflicts. Tension and anxiety result whenever workers are placed in compromising situa-

tions involving two or more sets of pressures. For example, if an employee is given a certain task to perform which causes another task to become more difficult or impossible to perform, the worker feels burdened or incompetent. These kinds of conflicts, if allowed to continue on a regular basis, lead to extreme anxiety, lowered self-confidence and self-esteem, and distrust of supervisors and fellow workers.

9. Don't promote beyond a worker's level of competence. Many stressful situations result when workers are promoted to positions for which they're unqualified because of poor education or lack of skills. We all have our own level of competence beyond which we can no longer perform effectively the things expected of us. Therefore, it's just as important to recognize workers who don't have the skills or abilities to do a job as it is to recognize the ones who do. Recognizing levels of competence is very important. Once a worker goes beyond that level, he or she will quickly become isolated, depressed, and insecure. The manager, in turn, has to compensate for the worker's inability by increasing his or her own work load or by spending time correcting or preventing mistakes. In the end, stress becomes a two-way street affecting both worker and manager.

To help eliminate job stress, managers should understand and respond to worker needs and then establish policies which reflect a concern for those needs. Small changes in attitudes, behavior, and treatment of workers has a big impact on the health and well-being of everyone, including the managers themselves. By actively practicing these kinds of stress relief strategies, managers, whose own stress levels are closely tied in with worker stress levels, will ensure that the overall environment is productive and stress free.

Expectations vs. Reality

There's no such thing as a perfect job. Whatever career we choose, whatever job we do, there will always be the problem of altering or adjusting our expectations to meet reality. This often happens when we get our first job, when we change jobs, or when we get promoted. Our enthusiasm and eagerness for work quickly disappears when the reality of work and the problems associated with it begin to surface. Instead of being the exciting, rewarding occupation we expected, we see that, in reality, our job can be downright dull. Whenever our expectations exceed job reality but don't reach a balance after a certain period of time, we begin to experience the stress of "unattainable expectations." Here's an example of how some expectations and job realities can differ and become a real source of job stress.

Expectation	Reality
Work will be a challenging, stimulating, and rewarding experience.	Work is more often routine and sometimes very boring.
We'll be asked to use all our educational training or all our skills to do our job.	Much of what we learn in school is not practiced on the job. We often learn to do things the company way.
We'll be needed to utilize our abilities and intelligence in decision making and in implementing new ideas.	Decision making and the implementing of ideas are left to senior executives and managers.

These are only some of the ways expectations and job realities don't match up in the real world. The first thing we need to realize is that the standards we set for ourselves are sometimes too high, even for good companies to meet. Being reasonable in what we expect from our work will make our adjustment to reality much easier. If we're not, the stress of unattainable expectations can easily lead to deflated enthusiasm, cynicism, total job dissatisfaction, and burnout. These, in turn, can cause serious job-related illnesses such as ulcers, hypertension, and coronary heart disease.

When reality finally sets in, how do we cope with the fact that our expectations may never be realized? Instead of becoming depressed and isolated, we can begin to adjust to reality by accepting three irrefutable facts of work life:

1. Expectations in all areas of life, including work, are almost always distortions of reality. Reality, then, is always going to be a disappointment at first unless we accept the challenge and do something positive about it.

2. In almost all instances, work is something we need to fit into, not the other way around. No one is going to mold a job to meet our needs or demands unless we're someone very special. Positive attitudes make us more flexible and allow us to fit into almost any situation we want.

3. No job, regardless of what it is, is going to satisfy us unless we adopt attitudes and behaviors that condition us to perceive job events the way we want to perceive them. We can choose to make work either a pleasant or unpleasant experience through the power of our mind, and we can lower our expectations and still receive satisfaction from our work by setting realistic goals and by coming to terms with our negative feelings and attitudes.

Our job expectations, then, can be as powerful as our perceptions. If we expect something good to happen, and it doesn't, we naturally perceive our job situation in a negative way. If our expectations are so high that we never attain what we expect, then we begin to condition ourselves to perceive everything in a negative way all the time. We build subconscious images that reinforce and shape our attitudes and behavior, and we eventually form habits that strengthen our negative feelings toward work. The result is classic "burnout syndrome." Bringing expectations in line with reality can be difficult, but if we condition ourselves to perceive and accept job reality in a constructive way, we can avoid the pitfalls of chronic stress and burnout.

Burnout

The term "burnout" is often used these days whenever we talk about job stress because it has become a major problem in many professional and nonprofessional occupations. Burnout, simply put, is a gradual process by which a once productive and committed worker loses all concern and interest in his or her job or profession. Victims of burnout often experience physical and emotional exhaustion, total lack of interest in work, and detachment from fellow workers. Burnout isn't really the same as stress; rather, it's the direct result of prolonged exposure to stressful work conditions and situations.

Although burnout can strike anyone, the individuals most vulnerable are the ones who deal with people on a daily basis.

Occupations in the high risk category, for example, are teaching, nursing, medicine, law enforcement, and social work. Workers in these occupations need to be especially wary of symptoms that indicate the early warning signs of burnout syndrome. Other jobs that promote burnout are ones in which workers do repetitive or routine tasks, never get positive feedback, or have much responsibility but little control. The types of individuals most susceptible to burnout syndrome are perfectionists, egotists, idealists, workaholics, and those who can't say no.

Burnout Rating Quiz

The following quiz is one way to rate how prone we are to burnout, or our "burnout index." Following the quiz is a scoring key and a list containing some common signs and symptoms that are associated with burnout or that are seen shortly prior to burnout.

		Seldom	Sometimes	Always
1.	I feel hostile or angry at work.	1	2	3
2.	I feel like I have to succeed all the time.	1	2	3
3.	I find myself withdrawing from co-workers.	1	2	3
4.	I feel like everything I'm asked to do is an imposition.	1	2	3
5.	I find myself increasingly insensitive or callous to clients, co-workers, or associates.	1	2	3
6.	Work has become very boring, tedious, and routine.	1	2	3
7.	I feel like I'm at a standstill in my career.	1	2	3

8. I find myself feeling nega-   1   2   3
    tive about work and focusing
    only on its bad aspects.

9. I find myself accomplishing   1   2   3
    less than I ever have before.

10. I have trouble organizing my   1   2   3
    work and my time.

11. I'm more short-tempered than   1   2   3
    I've ever been before.

12. I feel inadequate and power-   1   2   3
    less to make changes at work.

13. I find myself taking out my   1   2   3
    work frustrations at home.

14. I consciously avoid personal   1   2   3
    contact more than I ever have.

15. I find myself asking whether   1   2   3
    my job is right for me.

16. I find myself thinking nega-   1   2   3
    tively about work even when
    I go to bed at night.

17. I approach each work day with   1   2   3
    the attitude of "I don't know
    if I'm going to make it through
    another day."

18. I feel as if no one at work   1   2   3
    cares about what I do.

19. I find myself spending less   1   2   3
    time working and more time
    avoiding work.

20. I feel tired or exhausted   1   2   3
    at work even when I get
    enough sleep at night.

Scoring Key: 20–34
                No Burnout

                35–49
                Moderate Burnout (early
                warning signs)

                50–60
                Severe Burnout (need help &
                guidance)

Signs and Symptoms of Burnout

Absenteeism	Hostility
Alcoholism	Indifference
Anxiety	Insensitivity
Apathy	Irritability
Boredom	Isolation
Callousness	Job dissatisfaction
Conflicts with workers	Low morale
Cynicism	Malaise
Defensiveness	Marital problems
Disillusionment	Moodiness
Depersonalization	Negativism
Depression	Paranoia
Drug dependence	Pessimism
Exhaustion	Reduced Accomplishments
Family problems	Resentment
Fatigue	Sexual problems
Fault finding	Suicide thoughts
Frustration	Weakness
Hopelessness	Withdrawal

If we're on the road to burnout, we'll probably experience several of these symptoms before the final stage of burnout occurs. But no matter what the cause is, burnout always involves a pattern which leaves us de-energized and emotionally exhausted. Figure 4a illustrates how job stress, if not relieved, can lead to serious and often debilitating burnout syndrome.

Burnout is essentially the result of "unrelieved job stress." Whenever we feel trapped in our job or helpless to solve problems or conflicts, the reality of our helplessness causes frustration, anxiety and a feeling of powerlessness. This frustration is transmitted to the people we work with and results in a work environment that becomes unbearable and depersonalized. Here are two specific examples of how burnout syndrome can develop.

Nancy was a young nurse who graduated near the top of her class. She brought with her an enthusiastic desire to help her patients and was eager to do everything she could to become an ideal nurse. After all, as a youngster, Nancy was given a glamorous and idealistic picture of nursing, and she continued to have that picture in her mind while in school. Shortly after she began work, however, she encountered critical and ungrateful patients and physicians who treated her like a second class citizen. Her expectation of what nursing was really like was shattered. Gradually, Nancy began to develop negative attitudes about patients and doctors, became hostile and short-tempered, and started to withdraw from her co-workers. In the end, Nancy became so bitter, cynical, angry, and dissatisfied that she was a threat to her patients.

Bob became a teacher with the hopes of making a real impact on children's lives. He graduated with the idea of being the best educator he could be and leaving a lasting impression on his students. By his third year, Bob started to get frustrated at poor working conditions, a nonsupportive administration, angry and critical parents and undisciplined students. These realities began to take their toll. Bob lost his enthusiasm, developed negative feelings, came to classes unprepared, and became detached from his students and fellow teachers. Eventually, the profession Bob loved so much was making him so ill that he made the choice to switch careers.

Both Nancy and Bob went through the four stages or phases of burnout before they finally burned themselves out completely. Had they caught their burnout during the first three stages, they could have reversed the process and become happy and productive workers once again. Very few individuals, however, can reverse the burnout process entirely once they've remained in the fourth and final stage of burnout for any length of time. Here are the four stages of burnout syndrome. We need to be aware of each stage in order to recognize the warning signals that tell us there's danger ahead.

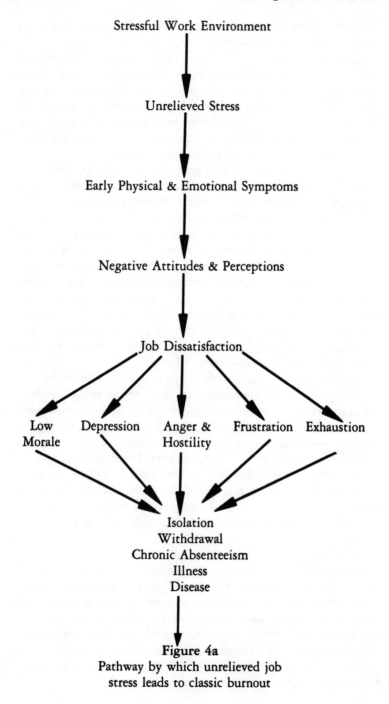

Figure 4a
Pathway by which unrelieved job
stress leads to classic burnout

Four Stages of Burnout Syndrome

Stage 1. *High Expectations and Idealism*

> Symptoms: Enthusiasm about the job
> Dedication and commitment to work
> High energy levels and accomplishments
> Positive and constructive attitudes
> Good outlook

Stage 2. *Pessimism and Early Job Dissatisfaction*

> Symptoms: Physical and mental fatigue
> Frustration and disillusionment
> Lowered morale
> Boredom
> Early stress symptoms

Stage 3. *Withdrawal and Isolation*

> Symptoms: Avoiding contact with co-workers
> Anger and hostility
> Severe negativism
> Depression and other emotional distress
> Inability to think or concentrate
> Extreme physical and mental fatigue
> Excessive amounts of stress symptoms

Stage 4. *Irreversible Detachment and Loss of Interest*

> Symptoms: Very low self-esteem
> Chronic absenteeism
> Terminally negative feelings about work
> Total cynicism
> Inability to interact with others
> Serious emotional distress
> Severe physical and emotional stress symptoms

Unless we've gone too far into the fourth and final stage of burnout, we can reverse the process through simple changes in our job goals, attitudes, and behaviors. There are some very effective coping strategies that are proven "burnout extinguishers." A few of them have been discussed in other chapters, perhaps in a slightly different way. We should read them again and again so they become a regular part of our stress management strategy.

Eleven "Burnout Extinguishers"

1. **Express feelings and emotions.** Putting stress into words through communication with colleagues can prevent the isolation often felt during the later stages of burnout. The exchange of ideas acts as a buffer because sharing and communicating has a unique way of relieving stress and putting things in perspective.

2. **Schedule down time.** Everyone needs breaks away from work. Instead of using lunch or coffee breaks to catch up on unfinished or extra work, spend down time doing something completely unrelated to work. Time off is absolutely essential in refreshing attitudes and job outlook.

3. **Recognize energy patterns and schedule work accordingly.** During a normal work day, we all have high and low levels of energy. Finding out when high energy levels occur and then scheduling stressful duties only during those times will prevent wear out and energy loss.

4. **Never schedule more than one stressful activity at the same time.** This may take some thought and planning beforehand, but putting up with only one stressful situation at any given time will prevent work pileup, make you feel like you're accomplishing more, and relieve the stress of feeling overworked.

5. **Engage in outside physical activities.** It's very important to participate in physical exercise because stimulating the body refreshes the mind. Our brain requires activity by the rest of our body in order to revitalize the senses and enhance performance. Exercise also builds physical resistance and makes us feel better about ourselves. When stagnation sets in, resistance and energy are lowered, and the natural tendency is to become more susceptible to physical and emotional distress.

6. Break projects down into smaller parts. Some of us have a tendency to become overwhelmed by a project soon after we start it. By cutting a big project down to its individual components, it never looks as difficult or overwhelming. We can then tackle it piece by piece and never even realize how big it is until it's finally done.

7. Delegate responsibility. If we're ever in a position to delegate responsibility to others, we should make it a point to do so. Rather than take on every problem that comes up, we need to allow others to share in problem solving and decision making.

8. Learn to say no. Never feel obligated to take on extra assignments or do special projects which aren't required but which cause feelings of anger and hostility. Saying yes all the time makes us feel helpless, while being able to say no gives us a feeling of control and satisfaction. This isn't the same as not wanting to get involved and committed. Giving ourselves the choice of what we want to be involved in or committed to is the kind of control we need to have to become stress free.

9. Improve work skills. We need to become more aware of new changes and keep abreast of current technologies and ideas. Taking classes, going to seminars and participating in extra job training will keep us up-to-date and prevent feelings of inadequacy. If we don't, we'll become more and more withdrawn and isolated. Eventually, our inability to work effectively with others will cause serious emotional problems.

10. Strive for success. Never be satisfied with doing only what you've been trained to do. Successful individuals learn new things, take risks, go out of their way to improve career goals, and are anxious to meet new and exciting challenges. If you're willing to extend yourself and reach for success, then chances are you'll never experience burnout.

11. Learn to relax. Set some time aside each day to bring your body back to a state of "relaxed equilibrium." Learning the art of conscious relaxation (discussed in a later chapter) will have a greater benefit than sleep and allow you to accept and cope with stressful situations more readily.

Two myths about burnout are that it occurs suddenly and that it only happens to workers in certain occupations. In reality, burnout can happen to anyone. It usually develops slowly and can take years before the symptoms of burnout manifest themselves as physical and emotional problems.

The good news is that it's easily recognizable and easily reversible during the first several stages. Dealing with burnout, however, requires both preventive action and stress reduction. Practicing the coping strategies discussed in this chapter attacks the root of job stress and job dissatisfaction caused by attitudes and behaviors. Using the relaxation techniques discussed in later chapters, together with these coping strategies, will make it easier to reverse the burnout process and help you experience a fuller and more rewarding work life.

Executive Job Stress

Executives and managers are susceptible to job stress in a unique way. They not only deal with subordinates, they deal with top management. This dual source of stress often makes the workplace a literal battlefield in which the executive is squeezed from both sides. And according to mortality data, this is one of the key relationships that causes many job-related health problems.

Another, and perhaps a more threatening, relationship that causes stress-related health problems is the relationship between a worker and an executive with an abusive or abrasive management style. The abusive or abrasive executive is a domineering or perfectionistic individual who finds it extremely difficult to be satisfied with other people's work. This creates a tense and severely stressful atmosphere which ultimately affects the executive through negative feedback, insubordination, isolation, and hatred.

Herbert Levison, a researcher who has studied the effects of management personality and style on work-related stress, postulated thirteen questions which, when answered honestly, should indicate whether or not someone has an abusive or abrasive management style.

1. Are you condescendingly critical? When you talk of others in the organization, do you speak of straightening them out or whipping them into shape?

2. Do you need to be in full control? Does almost everything need to be cleared with you?

3. In meetings, do your comments take a disproportionate amount of time?

4. Are you quick to rise to the attack; to challenge?

5. Do you have a need to debate? Do discussions quickly become arguments?

6. Are people reluctant to discuss things with you? When someone does, are their statements inane?

7. Are you preoccupied with acquiring symbols of status and power?

8. Do you weasel out of responsibilities?

9. Are you reluctant to let others have the same privileges or perquisites as yourself?

10. When you talk about your activities, do you use the word "I" disproportionately?

11. Do your subordinates admire you because you are strong and capable, or because in your organization they feel strong and capable—and supported?

12. To your amazement, do people speak of you as cold and distant when you really want them to like you?

13. Do you regard yourself as more competent than your peers or your boss? Does your behavior let them know that?

Executives who answer yes to several of these questions need to seriously reevaluate their attitudes toward workers. If left unchecked, abrasive and abusive management styles can create very intense stress and anxiety and affect the functioning and productivity of entire departments or organizations.

Executive Behavior Traits and Job Stress

Relationships between executives and workers are a major source of job stress. Experiences and behavior is another. In a study of 500 executives, it was shown that the executive especially at high risk was one who had experienced certain life events or who had certain personality and behavioral traits. In male executives, job stress manifested itself mainly as physical problems such as coronary heart disease and ulcers, while in female executives stress had a tendency to make them more susceptible to mental illness. In both male and female executives, however, the factor that most often appeared to bring on physical and mental health problems was Type A behavior. The ten factors that were seen more frequently in sick executives than any other factors were:

- Type A behavior pattern
- Lack of social support at work or at home
- Smoking heavily
- Drinking alcohol excessively
- Little or no exercise
- Experiencing negative life events
- Experiencing frequent life and work stress during the past ten years
- Having responsibility for many subordinates
- Frequent promotions
- Frequent relocations

These ten factors are really "precipitating agents" which enhance susceptibility to health problems. Executives who can identify with some of these factors are more prone to stress reactions and need to take extra steps to eliminate or at least moderate as many of these factors as they can.

In order to lessen the threat of executive stress syndrome, executives should improve their management styles as well as their relationships with subordinates. They should also take a close look at their personal lifestyles and try to eliminate those factors that enhance stress effects. All of these things can be made easier by following three guidelines. These are:

1. Identify the elements within the system that are causing stress. Because job stressors are often such a routine part of their work, executives must take the time to sit back and really think about specific tasks or situations that cause stress. Keeping a stress diary would be an ideal way to get started. Charting behavior patterns and physical symptoms is an easy method for pinpointing sources of job stress.

2. Decide on a plan of action. After identifying the elements that are causing stress, executives need to decide whether or not those elements can be changed or eliminated. Some sources of stress are just part of the job, and there's nothing anyone can do to change them. But it's often possiblt to reorganize schedules, shift work loads to peak energy times, utilize time management practices to become more efficient, set priorities, etc. Whatever method is used, it's important to make a decision and then begin a plan of action as soon as possible.

3. Follow through until stress is relieved. Once the source of stress is identified and a plan of action is decided on, stress becomes much more manageable. Any of the stress management strategies can be used—relaxation techniques, attitude adjustment, behavior modification or, in most cases, a combination of all three. The best way to fight stress is to use all the tools available in order to relieve job stress in the quickest and most effective way possible.

Every year, more than $50 billion is lost because of executive stress as a result of stress-related financial mismanagement, decreased worker productivity, inefficiency, illness, absenteeism, and premature death. More than ever, today's executive is at risk because the complexity of the workplace is so overwhelming. Dealing with stress by focusing on the reasons and the causes, and then alleviating that stress through various stress management strategies is critical for executives and their families. It's also critical for companies concerned about their workers' health and well being as well as their own future productivity and growth.

At any one time, ten to twenty percent of the total work force experiences physical and/or emotional health problems due to job stress. Reactions to stressful work situations depend on a number of things, the most important being distorted and unattainable expectations and negative perceptions about the job and how it affects us. Alleviating job stress can only be accomplished if we identify the elements within the system that cause stress and then actively pursue coping strategies that will channel our energies toward more positive and constructive attitudes.

Workers and managers together can implement beneficial changes, but the real challenge in successful job stress management is being able to recognize the situations that can be changed and the ones that cannot. Adjusting to the situations that cannot be changed through stress management techniques and strategies is the ideal goal each of us needs to strive for. The serenity prayer, written by Reinhold Niebuhr in 1934, reflects that goal and contains within it a philosophy to enable us to relieve many of our job-related stress problems and to help us lead happier and more productive lives.

> *O God, give us serenity to accept what cannot be changed,*
> *Courage to change what should be changed,*
> *And wisdom to distinguish the one from the other.*

5

Time Management

One of the biggest stress factors we face, whether it's at work or at home, is our inability to manage time. Time management, or the lack of it, creates stress because without time we loose the freedom to do what needs to be done, to be who we want to be, and to enjoy the things we want to do. We accomplish only what we can "fit into our schedules." And we find ourselves pressured because our lives and our work are constantly dictated by time.

Time management, then, allows us to organize our lives in a way that makes us happier and more productive; it gives us the ability to schedule ourselves into a normal day-to-day routine so we're left with the time we need for ourselves and our family; and it prevents chronic stress by eliminating the constraints we place on ourselves as a result of poor or inadequate organizational skills. After reading this chapter, we should be able to change some of our behavior patterns and manage ourselves more efficiently so that time becomes an ally rather than a culprit in our lives.

Behavior Patterns and Time Management

It's not the things we do during the day that create time problems, it's the way we do them. More often than not, the reasons for our inability to manage time are improper behavior patterns and attitudes. Behavior and attitudes can both be changed through proper techniques and conditioning. Both can be used as positive reinforcers that make us more efficient at utilizing the time we have. As a first step, however, we need to recognize those things about ourselves that cause time-related stress.

The following time quiz should help identify trouble spots and guide us toward our goal of becoming successful time managers. Read each statement carefully and circle the corresponding number that comes "closest" to answering the statement. (1 = Always; 2 =

Usually; 3 = Sometimes; 4 = Rarely) At the end of the quiz is a
scoring key which indicates levels of time management skills.

1. I find that I have enough   1   2   3   4
    time for myself—to do the
    things I enjoy doing.   1   2   3   4

2. I'm aware of deadlines and   1   2   3   4
    schedule my work to meet
    them in plenty of time.

3. I write down specific objec-   1   2   3   4
    tives in order to work toward
    goals.

4. I use a calendar to write   1   2   3   4
    down appointments, deadlines,
    things to do, general notes.

5. I feel in control of time   1   2   3   4
    while at work and at home.

6. I plan and schedule my time   1   2   3   4
    on a weekly and/or monthly
    basis.

7. I make a daily to-do list   1   2   3   4
    and refer to it several
    times per day.

8. I set priorities in order of   1   2   3   4
    importance and then schedule
    time around them.

9. I'm able to find blocks of   1   2   3   4
    time when I need them in case
    something important or extra
    has to be fit in.

10. I'm able to say no when I'm   1   2   3   4
    pressed for time.

11. I try to delegate responsi-   1   2   3   4
    bility to others in order to
    make more time for myself.

12. I organize my desk and work   1   2   3   4
    area to prevent clutter and
    confusion.

13. I find it easy to eliminate   1   2   3   4
    or reschedule low priority
    items.

14. I try to do things in a way   1   2   3   4
    that cuts down on duplicated
    effort.

15. I find that doing everything   1   2   3   4
    myself is very inefficient.

16. I try to shift priorities as   1   2   3   4
    soon as they change.

17. I find it easy to identify   1   2   3   4
    sources of time problems.

18. I find it easy to eliminate   1   2   3   4
    or reshuffle unnecessary
    paperwork.

19. My meetings and activities are   1   2   3   4
    well organized and efficient.

20. I know what I'm capable of and   1   2   3   4
    try not to overextend myself.

21. I find it easy to keep up with   1   2   3   4
    changes that affect my schedule
    or workload.

22. I know what my responsibili-   1   2   3   4
    ties and duties are.

23. I try to schedule the most   1   2   3   4
     difficult work during my most
     productive times.

24. I try to get only the perti-   1   2   3   4
     nent information before making
     a decision rather than try-
     ing to get as much information
     as possible.

25. I finish one job or task   1   2   3   4
     before going on to the next.

Scoring key: 25 - 40 = Excellent time manager
               41 - 55 = Good time manager
               56 - 100 = Poor time manager

After completing the quiz, we need to go back and identify those areas that are the most consistent sources of time-related stress. By recognizing the specific behavior patterns and attitudes that interfere with our ability to organize, manage, and schedule time, we can begin to reverse time management problems quickly and effectively. The most common areas to look for are:

- Not prioritizing tasks
- Not scheduling daily, weekly, or monthly activities
- Not delegating responsibility
- Not being able to say no
- Not writing down objectives in order to meet deadlines
- Not using a calendar to organize commitments
- Not shifting priorities to make room for more urgent tasks
- Not reducing clutter and unnecessary paperwork
- Not being able to give up total control
- Not being able to avoid procrastination

These are only the most common areas of poor time management. We all have our own individual weaknesses and, therefore, we need to recognize and eliminate those weaknesses by writing them down in a time management diary. The four areas that should be included in our diary are:

1. The event or activity.

2. Its priority ranking.
    1 = important
    2 = less important
    3 = least important
    4 = not important at all
3. The action we take.
4. A strategy for improving the way we handle the event or activity in order to enhance time management skills.

Time Management Diary

Time	Activity	Priority Ranking	Action Taken	Improvement Strategy
7:00				
7:30				
8:00				
8:30				
9:00				
9:30				
10:00				
10:30				
11:00				
11:30				
12:00				
12:30				
1:00				
1:30				

2:00				
2:30				
3:00				
3:30				
4:00				
4:30				
5:00				
5:30				
6:00				
6:30				
7:00				
7:30				
8:00				
8:30				
9:00				
9:30				
10:00				

A week of writing down activities and actions should be enough to indicate where time problems lie and what sorts of strategies can be taken to eliminate wasted effort. At the end of each day, write down "specific timewasters" and make a list of strategies that will solve problems dealing with those timewasters. Here's an example:

Timewaster	Strategy
Looking through every piece of mail.	Discard junk mail immediately. Put low priority mail aside until more time is available.
Having meetings that go on for a long time.	Make a meeting agenda and don't go beyond a specific time limit. Prepare better.
Having a lot of small duties that interfere with more important tasks.	Prioritize duties and/or delegate some of the lesser responsibilities to others. Eliminate unnecessary tasks.

Keeping a diary of activities and an accurate record of timewasters should give us a clear picture of how we're doing as time managers and how far we need to go to become ideal time managers. It's impossible to practice time management without first knowing what it is that makes us so poor at accomplishing a certain amount of work in a given amount of time. Once we put our finger on the problems and their sources, we can begin to adjust our daily behavior patterns in order to eliminate the root of our time-related stress. This is where conditioning and habit formation come into play once again. By consciously practicing good time management activities, we'll begin to break our old time management habits and condition ourselves to develop new and more effective behavior patterns.

In previous chapters, I've tried to emphasize the recurring theme of conditioning and habit formation as a powerful force in shaping our behavior and attitudes. Time management is no different. The skills we develop and the ways in which we organize our lives are made possible through positive reinforcement. Our brain responds to any kind of conditioning process in the same manner whether it's perceptions, behaviors, or attitudes. In this case, the positive reinforcer is our ability to accomplish something within the time limits we set for ourselves. For most of us, this in itself is a rewarding and satisfying experience. So, the more effectively we manage our time, the less stress we feel and the more positive the conditioning process becomes. Eventually, good time management becomes a permanent and natural part of our lives.

Fifteen Effective Time Management Strategies

Nothing comes easily at first. While we may think that changing the way we've done things will be simple, our habits will prevent us from becoming ideal time managers overnight. We need to put time management strategies into practice immediately and then stay with them. It's only through repetition that conditioning takes hold and begins to shape our behavior in the manner we choose. The following are fifteen ways to develop good time management habits and at the same time achieve our number one goal of eliminating time-related stress.

1. Write down weekly goals, plans, activities and objectives. At the beginning of each week, make a list—in writing—of all the things you're planning to accomplish by the end of the week. This may include special projects, recreational activities, assignments, meetings, etc. Force yourself to write down unpleasant goals as well as enjoyable ones. This initial "self-planning" session shouldn't turn out to be a concrete schedule, but rather a preliminary activity chart that can be referred to during regular planning and scheduling. This kind of tentative to-do list will get the wheels rolling and make further planning and scheduling much easier.

2. Prioritize tasks according to importance and urgency. After writing down activities, goals, and plans, give them a priority ranking. Which are top priority? Which are low priority? Which can be shifted or eliminated if more important events come along? Priority rankings can be given a numerical rating from 1 to 4 as follows:

    Priority #1   Top priority. Activity or task needs to be done as soon as possible. Plan your schedule around the activity in order to meet deadlines.

    Priority #2   High priority. Not as urgent as top priority, but should be done soon. Important enough to be put high on schedule.

    Priority #3   Low priority. Activity or task can wait until other higher priority activities are accomplished. Responsibility may be delegated to someone else if time is a factor.

> *Priority #4* Least priority. Not important or necessary. Activity or task should be placed last on the list, eliminated, or given to someone else to do.

3. Plan schedules in an organized manner by using calendars, appointment books, etc. Making use of a daily or weekly calendar is one of the best ways to help organize time and to plan schedules. There's nothing worse than jotting things down on loose pieces of paper or depending on your memory to keep activities straight. Calendars and appointment books are organized in a way that makes scheduling and planning easy, effective, and manageable.

4. Schedule the most demanding tasks during periods of highest energy. It's true that there are morning people, afternoon people, and night people. The most efficient individuals are the ones who recognize when their high energy levels occur and then adjust their schedules accordingly. In most cases, it's better to tackle the most demanding assignments first and leave the easier tasks for the end of the day. Scheduling work in this manner will make you feel good because you'll get the tough assignment out of the way and finish the day in a pleasant and refreshing way.

5. Eliminate timewasting activities. Make a list of all the things you do each day that are unnecessary and cost you time and energy. Activities like reading every piece of junk mail or talking to everyone who calls can take valuable time away from more important tasks and leave you frazzled by the end of the day. Make a commitment to eliminate the least important activities or, if necessary, put them at the end of the list.

6. Become a good delegator. In order to be a good time manager, you have to be a good delegator. One of the biggest causes of job stress comes from the attitude that you have to do it all yourself. Being in total control is ineffective because it puts the burden of doing everything on your shoulders. Take a good look at your daily and weekly schedule of activities, plans, and goals, and then decide which of those can be handled by someone else. If you're working longer

hours than everyone else, it's probably a sign that you're taking on a disproportionate amount of responsibility yourself.

7. Finish one task before starting another. It's very common to see someone trying to do several things at the same time. Some of us can handle that kind of routine; most of us can't. What happens is that things get started all the time and then put aside to be finished later. Before long, there are more unfinished tasks than finished tasks and we begin to feel the pressure of mounting work. Bad priority assignments and procrastination are the two biggest culprits. The rules to follow when faced with this kind of dilemma are:

    ●   Assign a priority rating to every task. Reschedule, postpone, or eliminate low priority tasks. Begin high priority tasks immediately.
    ●   Eliminate the tendency to procrastinate. Don't delay something because it's unpleasant or time consuming. If it needs to be done, start right away. Also, don't lump lengthy assignments together. Intersperse long assignments with short assignments to avoid boredom and fatigue.

8. Become a good note taker. Being able to solve problems, accomplish goals, or finish assignments might depend to a large extent on information you receive on the spur of the moment. Taking good notes helps you keep that information available when you need it. Good note taking is also helpful when jotting down things people tell you while you're away from your calendar or appointment book. So, always keep a pencil and small notepad in your pocket, handbag, or briefcase and get in the habit of using it.

9. Learn to say no. If you're a yes person, saying no may be one of the hardest things to do at first. But of all the time management strategies, learning to say no is one of the best ways to avoid scheduling problems, eliminate timewasting activities, and stay in control of day-to-day planning and organizing. Saying yes to everything is stressful because it makes you feel as if everyone but you is making the decisions about how you spend your time. If you feel uncomfortable

saying no outright, try this technique. When asked to do something, say "let me check my schedule and get back with you. I don't like to commit to anything unless I know that I can give 100 percent. "Later, check your schedule and decide if you're going to say yes or no. If you want to say no, explain your situation and leave it at that. By delaying your answer, you won't feel put on the spot and you'll be able to say no more easily. This delaying technique is very effective because it allows you to remove yourself from the situation and plan a strategy for saying no.

10. Leave 10 to 20 percent of your schedule open. Never fill up your schedule or calendar completely. Always make a block of time available each day for emergency meetings, unexpected jobs, or sudden schedule changes. Blocks of time are not to be used for lunch or regular breaks since these activities should already be programmed into your daily schedule anyway. If an open block of time gets used for some reason, analyze your schedule again and free up another block of time by eliminating a low priority activity or rescheduling it for another day. By leaving yourself with some available time each day, you'll become less anxious knowing that you'll always be able to schedule "just one more thing" if you really need to.

11. Develop an effective deadline strategy. Once you decide to do something, there are certain things you can do to make sure deadlines are met. These are:

> *Don't put off a project that has a specific deadline.* Procrastination just makes deadlines harder to meet.

> *Don't ignore deadlines.* Write them down, know when they are, and be aware of how long you have until the deadline ends. As long as you have a handle on deadlines, you can work toward those deadlines in an effective way.

> *Break the entire project down into smaller parts.* And set individual deadlines for each part. In this way, you can take it one step at a time and constantly judge how well you're doing along the way. Meeting deadlines consistently will make you feel productive and give you the incen-

tive and motivation to keep striving toward the final deadline. Breaking projects down really helps you stay on schedule because you'll be following a specific plan of action that keeps you on track.

Allow yourself a few minutes away from work every two hours or so in order to catch your breath and clear your mind. However, don't get in the habit of wasting time by taking breaks every thirty minutes to get a drink or stretch your legs. Set up a schedule of two hours work and ten to fifteen minutes of break and then stick with it.

12. Don't put off making decisions. Effective time management requires effective decision making. And effective decision making doesn't necessarily mean waiting until you have every fact and piece of information possible before making that decision. There comes a time when you have to say to yourself "I have the necessary information I need; I can act now without having to look at anything else and without wasting any more time." The tendency is, the longer you wait, the more information you want and the harder it is to make a final decision. The four steps to follow in order to avoid this are:

- Write down the decision you have to make.
- List the most important facts or the most important information you need to make a good decision.
- Get those facts and that information as quickly as possible.
- Make a decision based only on those facts and that information.

13. Improve reading and writing skills. Basic to all effective time management is the ability to read quickly and to write well. A good part of effective reading is knowing what to read, what to skim, and what to ignore altogether. If you can do that, you'll have less material to concentrate on and more time to do actual reading. Eliminating any unnecessary reading material right away will free up much of your time and give you a chance to fill your schedule with more important activities. Effective writing is necessary for time management because it allows you to spend less time think-

ing about how to write and more time thinking about about what to write. Both reading and writing can be improved through self-study or by taking some courses designed to enhance reading and writing skills.

14. Develop an effective reminder system. No one, regardless of how good they are at remembering things, can remember everything. This is especially true when it comes to following up on activities, jobs, or meetings. In cases where you have to be reminded to follow up on something, use a system that involves a daily check of all follow-up activities. For example, as soon as you decide to follow up on an activity, write it down on an index card along with the date you expect to act on it. Each day, check your index card file and make sure that your follow-up activities don't interfere with more important plans. Using reminder systems along with your daily and weekly schedules will keep you organized and efficient, especially when your work schedule is full and hectic.

15. Be in control of your activities and responsibilities. Being in control is as important in time management as it is in stress management. All the scheduling, planning, and organizing in the world isn't going to do any good if you can't keep control over disturbances, distractions, and other activities that are going to disrupt your day. In order to stay on top of activities and keep control, try avoiding the following:

Avoid spending too much time on the telephone. Talking on the telephone unnecessarily makes you lose touch of time and keeps you from staying on schedule. Rules to follow are:

- Don't answer your own phone if you can avoid it.
- Have important calls put through and respond to other calls only when you have free time.
- If you have to answer your own phone, decide on your response within the first 30 seconds. If the call is not urgent, say "I'll have to call you back. I'm in the middle of something urgent."

Avoid unnecessary socializing. While some socializing and taking breaks are essential for proper work attitudes, overdoing socializing and taking breaks is a waste of valuable time and can lead to bad habit formation. Spend ten to fifteen minutes every few hours away from your work. Control the tendency to lengthen breaks or take more frequent ones than necessary.

Avoid upward delegation. In order to fully control your schedule, you need to prevent people from delegating work back to you. Poor time managers have the problem of not being able to delegate work in a way that will keep it delegated until it's finished. Good time managers delegate responsibilities in order to free their schedules. They won't allow subordinates to delegate it back to them. Delegation goes hand in hand with control; the more effectively you delegate, the more in control you feel and the better you'll manage your time.

Avoid getting directly involved in others' activities. It's difficult to relinquish some responsibilities and duties, but in order to be in control of all your responsibilities, you can't allow yourself to continually get involved with everything everyone is doing. After delegating responsibilities to others, remove yourself from the situation and periodically check on progress. Being directly involved with every activity isn't necessarily a sign of commitment. It takes time away from more urgent and important duties and creates feelings of hostility and resentment between worker and manager.

Avoid unorganized meetings and discussions. Meetings should be well-planned and timed. Let people know exactly when the meeting will take place and how long it's going to last. Also, include some idea of what the meeting will be about and whether people should have something read or prepared beforehand. You need to have an agenda in front of you ready to go as soon as the meeting begins. If you and everyone involved are well prepared ahead of time, meetings and discussions can be kept under control and to the point.

6

Stress and Mental Health

Throughout history, mental health problems have often been depicted in stories about people being "possessed by demons" and acting in an "ungodly and unnatural way." The stigma of being different was so great that mental health was largely ignored for much of our history, and it wasn't until the later part of this century that we began to look more closely at mental health disorders. The reason for this was that with increasing modernization came increasing anxiety, depression, and psychoses. We started to discover that these and many other mental illnesses were often linked to the stresses and strains of a society that we ourselves had slowly created. As a result, stress is now regarded as one of the main causes of mental and emotional problems.

The reasons individuals develop mental health disorders are complex, and it would be simplistic to attribute all mental health problems to stress alone. But in this chapter, we'll see how mental health and stability can be deeply affected by the way we handle stress and by our ability or inability to manage that stress in a positive and constructive way. We'll also see how certain coping strategies are vital in relieving the emotional traumas and mental disorders directly caused by prolonged exposure to stress.

Stress and Depression

One day, Abraham Lincoln sat down and wrote to his law partner, John Stuart: "I am now the most miserable man living. If what I feel were equally distributed to the whole human family, there would not be one cheerful face on earth. Whether I shall ever be better, I cannot tell; I awfully forebode I shall not. To remain as I am is impossible. I must die or be better . . . "

Lincoln suffered from the same disorder that affects some 127 million people throughout the world and an estimated 9 to 11 million Americans at any given time. Depression—also known as clinical depression or depressive disorders—is the most prevalent mental health problem in the United States. As old as recorded civilization—ancient Egyptian manuscripts and writings of Greek physicians refer to it as "melancholia" or madness—depression respects neither social class, race, sex, nor ethnic group. Children as young as age 5 have been treated, but the peak years for depression are ages 25 to 44.

Psychiatrists consider many kinds of depression to be a response to emotional stress rather than a specific disease or illness. They treat it through individual coping strategies and various stress management techniques. In many cases, stress-related depression is cured by increasing social interaction, communication, and involvement. Social and moral support, then, can be very important in determining whether or not depression, as well as other mental health problems, develop at all.

Signs and Symptoms of Depression

According to the standard medical definition, depression is a syndrome which may involve mood variations, insomnia, weight loss, guilt, and lack of reactivity to one's environment. We all become depressed at one time or another, and we all exhibit different signs and symptoms of depression. Our depression can be something as simple as sadness or something as severe as deep withdrawal in which case we isolate ourselves and find it impossible to function normally. Here's a list of common symptoms of depression. We can use it as a guide to recognize certain traits and behaviors that are characteristic of depression.

Insomnia or excessive sleep
Compulsive behavior (overeating, anorexia, bulimia, etc.)
Withdrawal and isolation
Loss of control
Loss of memory and/or concentration
Disinterest in work or other activities
Physical pains (headaches, backaches, etc.)
Feelings of loneliness and/or emptiness
Frequent self-doubts and self-criticism
Irritability
Excessive alcohol or drug abuse
Loss of interest in sex
Thoughts of or attempts at suicide
Enduring feelings of sadness, guilt, or hopelessness

Depression as a Negative Stress Response

When we look at specific examples of mental health problems, we discover that stressful negative life events account for a large number of depression cases. In 1984, for example, when the stress effects of the Three Mile Island nuclear disaster were examined, it was found that one and a half years after the accident residents of the island exhibited more stress symptoms and reported more depression, anxiety, and alienation than residents living in outlying areas. In 1969, when a team of investigators looked at the life events of 185 depressed patients prior to the onset of their depression, they discovered that, in almost all cases, there was an overwhelming excess of negative life events or events involving some sort of personal loss. Many studies such as these have clearly demonstrated that depressed individuals experience more stressful life events in the months that precede the start of their depression. Moreover, the risk of depression is thought to increase five to six times during the six months following a tragic or severely stressful episode.

Stress events especially likely to cause depression are: loss of relatives or loved ones, loss of a job, relocation, severely threatening episodes, and chronically undesirable experiences. But in many cases, the stress events that cause depression are small, repetitive occurences rather than major stress events. The cumulative effect of these "microstressors" can be equally, if not more, potent than the major or "macrostressors" because of their frequency and their repetitive effect on conditioning and habit forming processes. At times, in fact, they've proven to be much more damaging due to the prolonged effect they have on our physical well-being and on our mental ability to adjust and cope.

Regardless of its cause, depression makes us repeat our symptoms over and over again, leaving us open to negative conditioning and habit formation that will perpetuate the depression. Unless we put into practice strategies for reversing or coping with depression, our habits will become harder to break and could remain with us throughout life. But if there's one positive side to depression, it's that, in almost every case, it's easy to recognize. The signs and symptoms of depression are a warning signal that tell us our stress response has gone overboard and is beginning to cause serious problems. These early warning signals allow us to deal with our stress immediately and effectively before depression slips into a dangerous and chronic stage.

Becoming Depression Resistant

Perhaps the single most important factor that separates a depression prone individual from a depression resistant one is the former's inability to cope effectively with negative life stresses. Once depression prone individuals learn coping strategies, many of them begin to lead normal, healthy lives. For instance, it was shown that patients at a community mental health center, who participated in a 30-hour program designed to teach relaxation exercises, social skills, and attitude and behavior modification, had significantly lower levels of depression and more ability to solve problems and control their lives than individuals who didn't participate in the program. Other studies have shown that depression increases as the number of stress events increase but decreases as the number of relationships and social interactions increase.

One of the best examples of how this kind of social support contributes to stress-related mental health is taken from the health records of ethnic groups in America. When an ethnic group forms a large community and, thus, has a substantial social support network, hospitalization rates due to mental health problems are very low. On the other hand, when an ethnic group begins to constitute a small minority of a neighborhood, the rates of mental illness and hospitalization begin to increase dramatically. The reason for this is that social support systems act as buffers against many of the stressful life events that we as individuals aren't able to deal with alone.

Social support and interaction are an essential part of stress management because they have such a positive effect on reversing the cycle of depression. In essence, when we become stressed, we need other people for interaction, communication, and social support. It's much easier to cope with or forget about our stress problems when we have someone to share with or some group to belong to.

Unless depression is severe and caused by deep emotional problems, certain coping strategies can be used to reverse or lessen depression syndrome. Here are four main coping techniques that are very effective in treated stress-related depression:

1. Increase social contacts and interactions with friends and family. Even if you have to force yourself to do so, make an effort to broaden your circle of friends. Then make it a priority to see them on a regular basis. It has been proven that stress and depression decrease as interactions increase.

2. Improve communication between yourself and others. This is especially true of verbal communication between a husband and wife or between a parent and child. Communication opens doors and makes relationships grow. Stress is much easier to handle when it's communicated than when it's left to fester inside of us. Whenever problems arise that create tense and stressful situations, express your feelings in a constructive and positive way. Here are some tips on how to do that.

   Don't dwell on negative things. Don't be self-critical. Make it a "mutual" dialogue.

   Write letters. Letter writing can be a very effective method of expression if verbal dialogue is difficult at first. Writing feelings down an paper makes them easier to discuss because they're physically in front of you.

   Learn to be a good listener. Listening is extremely important in good communication because it shows that you're interested in what the other person is saying. While listening, make eye contact because eye contact shows that you're paying attention and that you're concerned. Don't respond or talk too quickly. Always give the other person a chance to finish what he or she is saying. A mutual dialogue, not a lecture, is the most effective way to communicate.

   Avoid nonpertinent issues. Don't bring up any past grievances or troubles you've had even if they deal indirectly with the present discussion. If you know that certain issues are going to cause anger and resentment, don't bring them up deliberately or in a negative way.

   Focus on the underlying issue that's causing the problem. Talk about one thing at a time. Keeping to one topic prevents other issues from complicating the picture and making communication more difficult.

3. Develop social support systems. Social support systems may include a group of friends, your community, your church, or your family. There's no doubt that this one strategy can greatly brighten your outlook on life and help lessen depression and anxiety. Social support networks are used extensively by psychiatrists and psychologists to help treat mental health

problems because they've proven to be one of the best methods for enhancing relationships, communication, and interactions.

4.   Become involved. Taking part in activities, events, organizations, and social groups will get your mind off the source of stress and, at the same time, give you a sense of worth and self-esteem. Many depressed individuals find that involvement alone is the answer to their stress and to many of their mental health problems.

Coping strategies used for treating depression include the same kinds of attitude and behavior changes I prescribed earlier in the book. But, as with any health problem, the best treatment for depression really depends on the personality and character of the individual and the extent of depression. Depression can be a serious mental illness requiring drug therapy and extensive counseling. Often, a professional counselor or psychiatrist is needed to help decide which treatments are best. Severely depressed individuals should seek that professional help if they feel unable to solve their own problems. Learning to cope with stress and depression by using all the channels available is the best way to bring about a healthy and lasting recovery.

Stress, Depression, and Suicide

During the last few decades, individuals of all ages have been committing suicide at an alarming rate. According to sociologists, a large portion of these suicides are either directly or indirectly attributed to the mounting pressures and stresses of our society. We're affected by stress directly, for example, if we're exposed to pressure on the job. We're affected indirectly if our spouse is exposed to stress and he or she affects us. Either way, mounting emotional strain can be a very negative experience and lead to depression and self-destructive behavior.

In a study of highly prone suicidal women, it was found that they experienced intensely negative life stress, had a range of negative emotions, and were less interested and responsive to people. In another study, a close relationship was found between the stress of recession and suicide rates. For every 1 percent increase in unemployment, there had been 326 additional suicides per year. Both men and women are equally susceptible to the kinds of stresses that lead to suicidal behavior.

Recently, it was discovered that as many as 50 percent of all childhood and adolescent suicides may be disguised to appear as accidents. Since 1960, suicides for young people between the ages of fifteen and twenty four have gone up nearly 300 percent! Five thousand adolescents die each year from suicides, but the frightening reality is that another 50,000 to 100,000 will attempt suicide unsuccessfully. The only reason why suicide remains the number two cause of adolescent death is that it's impossible to prove fatal car accidents (the number one cause of adolescent death) are a means of committing suicide.

In many of these suicide cases, depression was found to be the main component that triggered the suicide in the first place. Depression in these young people is usually the result of negative life events, most notably a high prevalence of broken homes, divorce, or separation. When suicide prone college students were surveyed, the reasons found for intending suicide were: high levels of severe life stress, hopelessness, and high levels of depression. Poor problem solvers exhibiting these symptoms were especially at high risk.

Signs and Symptoms of Adolescent Suicidal Behavior

As adults, we tend to view adolescence as a period of friction, change, and problems. For the teenager, it's a very stressful time of concern about weight problems, acne, menstruation, late or early development, sexual arousal, school pressure, boredom, parental hassles, peer pressures, and money problems. It's a time of confused feelings, particularly in relationships with parents. Teenagers fight for independence, yet fear too much freedom; they resent overprotection but need and want parental attention. Because the adolescent years are such a trying period, we often fail to recognize certain signals that indicate suicidal feelings or thoughts. Many times, these signals are a cry for help. Here are some warning signs to look for.

- Isolation and withdrawal from people, especially close friends
- Sudden or gradual loss of interest in appearance
- Unusual change in grades, school work, tardiness, or attendance
- Loss of weight and/or appetite
- Insomnia or excessive sleep
- Self-criticism, low self-esteem, feelings of failure, or sense of worthlessness

- Preoccupation with death and/or dying
- Loss of interest in previous activities and involvements
- Sudden accident proneness
- Sudden change in personality, especially involving apathy and depression
- Sudden angry outbursts, irritability, and hostility
- Excessive use of alcohol or drugs
- Sudden acts of risky or dangerous behavior like speeding in a car or running across a busy street
- Feelings of hopelessness or helplessness
- Suddenly giving away valuable or prized possessions
- Actual threats or verbal cues about not wanting to live anymore

Not all teenagers react in the same way to painful or stressful situations. Likewise, because not all teenagers have the same coping skills and abilities, they'll all behave differently during tough times. But regardless of what kind of signal a teenager is transmitting, you can be sure that he or she is subconsciously pleading for help, guidance, and reassurance.

According to a study at the Vanderbilt University Division of Adolescent Medicine, there are certain "stress factors" that adolescents experience most frequently but that parents, teachers, and physicians are not very sensitive to. These stress factors can easily lead to depression, isolation, maladjustment, and/or suicidal feelings. The Vanderbilt study found 20 stressful life events that were most frequently reported by adolescents ranging in age from 11 to 19 years. The most common stress factors, in order of greatest frequency, were:

1. Making failing grades on report cards.
2. Increased arguments between parents.
3. Serious family illness.
4. Broke up with boyfriend/ girlfriend.
5. Death in family.
6. Problems with siblings.
7. Increased arguments with parents.
8. Failed grade.
9. Loss of close friend.
10. Personal illness or injury.
11. Change in family financial status.
12. Problems with classmates.

13. Changed to new school.
14. Teacher problems.
15. Parents divorced.
16. Mother/father lost job.
17. Friend experienced serious illness.
18. Brother/sister leaves home.
19. Moved to new home.
20. Death of close friend.

For parents and teachers, it's a challenge to keep a balanced perspective on the teenager's emotional roller coaster ride. As young people bounce back and forth between childhood and adulthood, alternating irresponsibility with responsibility, parents and teachers don't often know what to expect. For this reason, it's even more important to be on a constant lookout for adolescent stress factors and for emotional and behavioral symptoms that may indicate trouble ahead.

Communication and Involvement:
The Keys to Suicide Prevention

The problem of stress-induced child and teenage suicide is especially tragic because, in many cases, the warning signs of depression and suicide are very evident but often overlooked. It's extremely important for families to realize that lines of communication have to remain open between parent and child. If a young person knows that the home is a place where feelings can be expressed freely and ideas shared and exchanged without criticism, that person will be able to deal with stress and depression in a more positive way. As the results of a questionnaire given to adolescents showed, most chose "talking to a friend" as the single most important act they could do to lessen the threat of suicide. Communication is the key. If we can put stress into words, we can begin to interact with one another and develop a bond that will have a tremendous effect on our ability to cope.

When asked about specific problems with parents, teenagers most often cite "not being listened to" as a major source of frustration and anger. Really listening to and communicating with teenagers is difficult and can sometimes be near impossible. But even though adolescence is a trying period, parents and teenagers must keep tuned in to each other to overcome one of the most difficult times in life. Here are some suggestions that can help keep those lines of communication open.

- Give your undivided attention when your teenager wants to talk to you. Don't watch TV, fall asleep, or busy yourself with other tasks.

- Try to listen calmly, even though there may be a great difference of opinion. Concentrate on hearing and understanding your teenager's point of view. Don't start preaching when a give-and-take discussion is wanted.

- Develop a courteous tone of voice in communication. Respect brings respect—even in the way we speak. If we talk to our offspring as we talk to other people, our own youngsters might be more willing and likely to seek us out as confidants. Gruffness or abruptness arouses hostility, whereas a pleasant tone of voice pays great dividends in improved relationships.

- Avoid making judgments. Anyone stops confiding in somebody who's critical of his or her behavior. It's not necessary to approve all of your teenager's behavior, but it is important to understand the feelings involved. Putting yourself in another's place isn't always easy, particularly as attitudes, pressures, and choices change. It's a challenge for a parent to be firm about important values while being flexible enough to bend with changing times.

- Keep the door open on any subject. Too often, teenagers avoid discussing things that may make their parents feel uncomfortable. Belittling, humiliating, and laughing at youngsters can cause deep wounds and short circuit the lines of communication. Teenagers often pay a very high price for not having the right information about many subjects, including sex.

- Permit expression of ideas and feelings. Many young people have their own ideas about morality, marriage, work, education, time, money, and whatever else is a part of our way of life. Just because their views and philosophies are different from yours doesn't always mean they feel certain about them. Often, young people "test" their ideas in conversation. To communicate, you must be willing to listen first and acknowledge their opinions, even if you're alarmed by them. Then give your viewpoints as plainly and honestly as you can, recognizing that love and mutual respect can exist, even when points of view are different.

- Encourage positive self-worth. While you talk to your teenagers, build their confidence by encouraging (but not forcing) participation in sports, music, art, dance, or any other hobby or interest. Your youngster's new interests will usually be an added source of conversation and sharing.

- Be aware of how you treat other children in the family. Do you show favoritism? This could make another child feel rejected, unloved, and jealous. Try to be fair and consistent. It will pay off.

- Make an effort to say nice things. Too often, parents tend to focus on poor performance and behavior. Every human being needs acceptance and appreciation.

- Hold family conferences. Most teenagers feel they have little or no voice in family affairs. Family gatherings offer an excellent opportunity for children to participate in decision making and to work things out together.

In addition to improving communication, there are actions that parents can take to help their adolescents through the teenage years. Like communication, involvement and caring are important ingredients for decreasing stress and for making life more pleasant. The old saying, "actions speak louder than words," is particularly appropriate where parental influence on children is concerned. Here are some suggestions on what parents can do.

- Try to set a good example. Children learn by what they see. Too often, people say one thing and do another. "Do as I say and not as I do" won't carry much weight. Eventually, children will ask such questions as "What's wrong with taking drugs when my parents are getting stoned on alcohol?."

- Supervise and guide. Although teenagers are capable of handling certain privileges and responsibilities, they still need help in setting limits on their freedom and behavior. Deciding with the teenager what these limits and policies are usually elicits more reasonable attitudes. Moderate and selective guidance is one of the best ways to prevent a breakdown of communication.

- Communicate, in words and actions, what you expect of your children. Although teenagers may appreciate a share in some decision making, they don't want parents to give up authority or be wishy-washy. Parents who appear confused about firmness and discipline, who are inconsistent, or who disagree between themselves are perceived as weak and divided. Teenagers need the security of knowing where their parents stand and what parents expect of them.

- Respect the adolescent's desire for individuality and independence. Parents do, and should, attempt to influence their children. But this is quite different from trying to force them into preconceived molds to fit parents' desires. Parents can accept and respect their teenagers as individuals without accepting all their ideas. The reverse is also true; teens can maintain respect for parents while rejecting some of their beliefs. One expert in family problems suggests that parents assume the role of watchful bystanders, ready to come forward when help or guidance are needed.

- Take an interest in your children's activities and friends. This helps reduce the distance between the generations, since it demonstrates your acceptance of their world. Give the youngsters time to be with their friends and make their friends welcome when they come to visit. Taking an interest in your children's activities and friends doesn't mean taking on the role of a buddy or invading your youngster's privacy. Teenagers need time alone and privacy, just as parents do.

- Try not to overreact. Many parents brace themselves for the onslaught of adolescence, convinced that it's bound to be a long, hard struggle. Consequently, they're quick to overreact the first time their teenager steps out of line. They punish severely, withdraw trust, and lose confidence in the youngster, thus severing the lines of communication. It's only natural for adolescents to test their parent's authority while trying to assert themselves. At the same time, they're trying out their own competence. Parents must let their children make mistakes and at the same time be ready to help when help is needed.

How Teenagers Can Help

What responsibilities do teenagers have in decreasing the stress of adolescence and in bridging the generation gap? The following code of communication was formulated with the assistance of young people and adults. Parents and teachers have used this as an effective means to initiate or reopen the lines of communication. Have your child read the code, tell him or her that it was written with the help of teenagers, and then talk about it. Giving your teenagers the responsibility of helping with communication shows trust and confidence.

1. The first barrier of communication which I must cast aside is the attitude of ignoring anybody over 30. If I expect people to tune in to me, then I must be willing to talk to them.

2. Our generation wants understanding from our elders. In turn, it's only fair that we try to understand them. They have needs and feelings and reasons for their decisions.

3. I will listen to my parents with an open mind and look at the situation from their point of view. That's the way I would expect them to treat me.

4. I will share more of my feelings with my parents. They may have experienced some of the same problems. I need to give them a chance to help me.

5. I want my parents to express trust and confidence in me, to grant me more freedom and responsibility as I mature. It's necessary, then, that I live up to their confidence. What I do reflects on them, and they are held accountable for my actions and behavior.

6. Exercising the right to criticize my family, school, friends, or society includes the responsibility to suggest how practical improvements can be made.

7. To promote better communication in my family, I will practice courtesy and consideration for others. I will let my parents know I care about them. They're affected by pressures and problems of everyday living just as I am.

8. When I have a problem that I feel I can't handle, I won't keep it to myself. I'll be responsible enough to talk it out with my parents, and in return, they'll treat me with the respect and dignity I deserve.

According to many suicide studies, the high risk factors responsible for most of the suicides committed each year are severe depression, anxiety, hostility, and isolation/withdrawal, not necessarily in that order. For adolescents, there may be problems at school, with friends, with family or relatives, with moving, with personal conflicts, etc. Some of us are more vulnerable to these kinds of emotional problems than others. We become more unstable and susceptible during times of extreme stress. In order to minimize that vulnerability, it's very important to use coping strategies like taking up hobbies, participating in sports and activities, and being involved with friends and groups. The bottom line is to develop a way of handling emotional crises and stressful situations in a positive way as they come up. By far, the four areas that are most effective in doing this are:

1. Developing personal relationships.
2. Becoming involved in community, school, or religious organizations.
3. Increasing family and social interactions.
4. Increasing communication.

By channeling our efforts toward these areas, we'll begin to cope with stress more easily and for longer periods of time. We'll also be able to focus attention on the positive aspects of our lives and our children's lives and begin to view stress as something that we can control within ourselves.

Diet, Stress, and Depression

New research being done at medical centers around the country indicates that some cases of depression may be caused by nutrition and diet. It's now known that individuals can become depressed if they have a deficiency of either serotonin or noradrenaline in their brain. Stress, fatigue, and overwork deplete noradrenaline, resulting in emotional strain, lack of concentration, and loss of energy and vitality. Both serotonin and noradrenaline (also known as norepinephrine) act as nerve transmitters which send messages from the brain to the rest of the body. When these transmitters are blocked or impaired, our normal brain and bodily functions are seriously impaired. In addition, serotonin is released from platelets (small disklike structures in the blood) during an injury and causes smooth muscles to constrict and reduce blood flow. Figure 6a illustrates the pathway through which dietary proteins are converted to serotonin and noradrenaline.

Serotonin and noradrenaline are derived from amino acids found in meats, dairy products, and other food supplements. The dietary amino acid tryptophan is especially important because it's one of the 10 "essential" amino acids—essential because our body can't manufacture it and, therefore, must be consumed daily in our diet. Another amino acid—tyrosine—is also important because it's one of the building blocks of noradrenaline. In some cases, depressed patients have improved with tryptophan treatment while in other cases, patients have improved with tyrosine treatment.

The relationship between stress, depression, and serotonin is important because one of the vital functions of serotonin is to induce drowsiness and sleep. Sleep, in turn, is a very effective mechanism for helping us relax and for alleviating symptoms of depression. In some cases of depression, insomnia prolongs the amount of time spent dwelling on problems. Hence, sleep can be a good stress reliever and is critical in improving overall physical and psychological well-being.

Though the exact reason for sleep isn't well understood, we do know that lack of sleep for prolonged periods can produce irritable and neurotic behavior. It also makes us more susceptible to stress and stress reactions. Sleep, therefore, brings our body back to a state of balance and makes us more resistant to stress effects. By increasing tryptophan intake, which affects the production of serotonin, diet-induced depression might be alleviated or reversed altogether. Besides meats, the foods highest in tryptophan content are: milk, cheese, eggs, fish, dates, barley, beans, chickpeas, cowpeas, lentils, whole peas, and soybeans.

Depression due to low levels of noradrenaline can be treated by increasing the consumption of the amino acid phenylalanine, which is converted by the body into tyrosine. The foods highest in phenylalanine content are basically the same as they are for tryptophan. Phenylalanine supplements, however, should not be taken without the advice of a physician since they may have adverse side effects in people with hypertension.

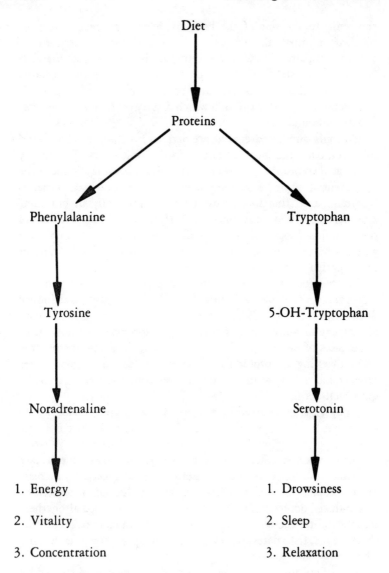

Figure 6a
Pathway through which dietary protein
is converted to serotonin and noradrenaline.

Antidepressant Drugs and Stress Reactions

Since ancient times, healers have put faith in medicines or drugs to cure mental illness. Potions, mineral baths, crushed herbs, vapors, and bromides have all been tried. But the successful breakthrough came in the 1950s with the development of antidepressants and tranquilizers. Since then, the prescription of antidepressant drugs has become a multimillion dollar business. According to a survey by the National Institute of Mental Health, more than 20 million prescriptions for such drugs are filled in any given year.

Antidepressant drugs can cause stress reactions for two reasons: (1) Because depression is such a complicated disorder, affecting individuals in many different ways, certain antidepressants can have side effects which create severe anxiety and physical disability, and (2) because some antidepressants need to be taken for as long as six weeks before they begin to work, depressed individuals may become discouraged or impatient and stop taking the drugs. This causes further depression and stress because they feel as if nothing can help them.

Most of these antidepressant drugs fall into three major classes: lithium, tricyclic drugs, and MAO inhibitors. Each can cause severe emotional stress by interfering with normal bodily functions, which in turn trigger physical stress reactions. Anyone taking antidepressants should report any kind of adverse side effect to his or her physician. In many cases, changing the drug or the dosage can relieve symptoms. Here are descriptions of each class of antidepressant drug:

Lithium: Lithium is a drug recommended for patients suffering from manic depression which involves incredible highs, unusual bursts of energy, aggression, and delusions of grandeur. A young people's disease, this depression most often strikes those in their mid-20s. Side effects of lithium may include nausea, lethargy, thirst, greatly increased urination, and possible weight loss.

Tricyclic drugs: Tricyclics are the most widely used class of antidepressant drugs. People using these drugs suffer from depression which involves insomnia, loss of appetite and weight, loss of energy, decreased ability to feel pleasure, suicidal thoughts, and thoughts of hopelessness and excessive guilt. Usually known as "classic depression," this depression most often strikes people in their late 30s or early 40s. Side effects of tricyclics may include irregular heartbeat, disturbed vision, sweating, dizziness, decreased or increased sexual desire, and constipation.

MAO inhibitors: These antidepressants are usually prescribed for people who haven't responded to tricyclics or else have "atypical" depression. Less typical than classic depression, this condition includes high levels of anxiety, phobia, and obsessive-compulsive behavior. Some individuals also sleep and eat a lot—in contrast to the insomnia and loss of appetite associated with classic depression. When mixed with beer, red wine, chocolate, pickled fish, cheese, yogurt, caffeine, and allergy pills, MAO inhibitors can trigger very high blood pressure, rapid pulse, headaches, problems with vision, even paralyzing or fatal strokes.

Clinical depression may be precipitated by the same losses and stresses that trigger "normal" depressed feelings. When antidepressant drugs cause side effects, they may actually create spontaneous stress reactions that further aggravate the depression. If you're one of the millions of people suffering from some form of depressive disorder, you need to be aware of antidepressants as a possible source of additional physical and mental health problems.

Stress and Schizophrenia

Schizophrenia is actually a group of mental disorders related to the thinking process. It includes symptoms such as delusions, hallucinations, and extreme withdrawal from society and other people. Like depression, schizophrenia may have a number of different causes including environmental factors and genetic predisposition. In many cases, however, people on the verge of schizophrenia have been shown to experience severely stressful events which precipitate and trigger the disorder.

As early as the 1930's, studies have shown that symptoms of schizophrenia are experienced by people whose lives are affected by the stresses of their lifestyles. For example, hospitalization rates for schizophrenia were highest among individuals living in the inner city, but decreased substantially for those who moved farther away into rural areas. Schizophrenia rates were also highest for low-status occupations in contrast to high-status occupations. This was especially true in cases involving minority immigrants who were poorly educated and spoke little or no English. Most recently, it was discovered that people with acute schizophrenia experienced certain kinds of serious crises and life changes in the 13 weeks prior to the onset of their illness, and that long-term tensions and anxiety in the home increased their chances of becoming schizophrenic. Even patients who had recovered from schizophrenia had relapses following stressful events and negative life change.

In the past, stress wasn't even considered a factor in the development of schizophrenia. It's now believed that individuals who are vulnerable to schizophrenia may succumb to it because stress actually precipitates it. And even though many cases of schizophrenia are caused by something other than stress, we can't ignore the fact that stressful life events are commonly found prior to the onset of the disease itself. Standard therapy usually involves the participation of family members, relatives, and social support groups.

The emotional stress associated with being the parent, spouse, or relative of a schizophrenic can be even greater than the stress experienced by the schizophrenic. Because of this, the benefits of support groups for family members are enormous. In these groups, stress is relieved by putting problems into words and talking about them. Often, high tension events are defused because individuals are once again able to cope with situations that they couldn't deal with alone. Social support is an important part of schizophrenia treatment because it involves relationships and activities which act as buffers against stressful life events.

Stress and Sexual Dysfunction

One of the leading causes of sexual problems in both men and women is emotional stress. In many cases, simply recognizing the stressor that's creating sexual problems is enough to bring about complete recovery. On the other hand, failure to recognize stress as a cause or as a contributing factor can lead to serious emotional disorders such as chronic guilt, depression, anxiety, and permanent loss of sexual desire.

It's well established that any kind of prolonged stressful physical or mental experience affects the concentration of sex hormones. That's because, during stress, our body must keep producing large amounts of stress hormones and, as a result sacrifices the production of sex hormones. In order to fight stress, our body shuts down our sexual mechanisms so we're better able to deal with more urgent and immediate needs. This change in the type of hormone produced has been called the "stress-shift in hormone production." Given the choice of responding to life-threatening situations or maintaining sexual activity, our body will almost certainly opt to protect itself first. This defense against stress is usually accompanied by some degree of sexual deficiency. Figure 6b illustrates the common pathway through which both stress hormones and sex hormones are produced.

In the male, both sex hormone and sperm production can be severely inhibited as a result of stressful experiences. Therefore, not only is the sex drive lowered, but fertility is significantly decreased because the ability to fertilize the ovum depends to a great extent on the total number of sperm cells produced. A number of years ago, a friend of mine experienced this phenomenon first hand. While living in New York City, we both worked in a very stressful environment. He and his wife tried unsuccessfully for six years to have a child. Two months after being transferred to another state, he called to say his wife was pregnant. Couples who are unable to have children, but are otherwise healthy in every way, may have to examine their lifestyles more closely before giving up their dream of having children altogether.

Although an imbalance between sex and stress hormones can play a role in causing sexual problems, the major factor is almost always the negative mental attitude created by stress itself. The three most common sexual problems that fall into this area are impotence, frigidity, and premature ejaculation. All three are usually the end result of fear, anxiety, tension, depression, or stressful life events. And all three can easily be cured through the use of stress management techniques, attitude adjustments, behavior modification, and special exercises that condition the brain and the genital muscles to respond in a normal way.

Sexual problems are especially stressful because they tend to spiral into a vicious cycle that grows worse and worse over time. Couples begin to find ways to avoid intimacy in order to avoid stress. But the stress becomes compounded because one or the other starts to feel rejected and isolated. The only way to end this stress cycle is to communicate feelings and anxieties and to realize that the problems may easily be reversed. If the source of sexual problems is indeed stress, then it would help to remember these things:

● Most sexual activity is under the control of the autonomic or involuntary nervous system. Any negative thoughts, emotions, or feelings (anxiety, tension, fear, guilt, shame, anger, embarrassment, etc.) will invariably trigger the brain to respond by shutting down all or most sexual mechanisms or

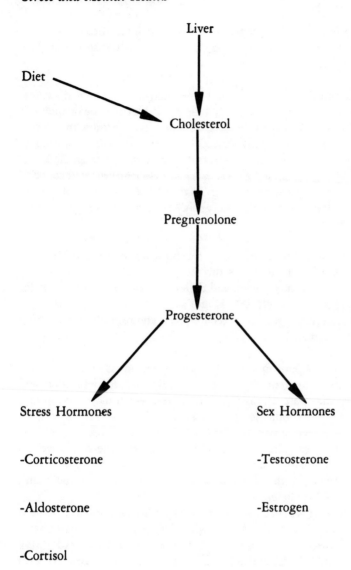

Figure 6b
Common pathway through which stress
hormones and sex hormones are produced

pathyways. These negative emotions are intensified every time a sexual problem occurs and, thus, a vicious conditioning cycle begins.

● Communication is the first step. Anyone experiencing sexual problems can become very lonely and hostile if he or she can't share feelings with someone. Couples have to know that sexual problems are usually caused by stress and that they need to become partners in the treatment. A man or woman alone can seldom overcome the cycle of sexual deficiency without cooperation from his or her partner. In many cases, the relief of sharing the stress, fear, and anxiety with a partner is enough for complete recovery.

● Use special exercises to help reverse sexual problems. There are several excellent books on the market which discuss sexual problems, their causes, and their cures. In these books, look for techniques such as "Kegel's exercises," "sensate focus technique," "stop-start technique, " and techniques for curing "performance anxiety."

Sexual problems in themselves are a tremendous source of stress. Becoming impotent or frigid can easily lead to depression and anxiety and cause illnesses such as ulcers, which may develop into more serious problems. It's impossible to say how many good marriages have broken up because couples didn't realize just how much stress can affect their sex lives. If there's one action we can take, it's to include our spouse or be included by our spouse in order to gain the strength needed to overcome a problem that usually can't be dealt with alone.

Whenever we encounter a stress-related sexual problem, we need to remember three things: (1) with high expectation comes occasional failure; (2) with occasional failure should come understanding, compassion, and a sense of unity; and (3) with understanding and unity comes communication and a deeper awareness of one another's needs. It's only through understanding, compassion, and communication that we truly begin to rid ourselves of the sexual problems that are driven by negative stress responses. If we can do that, we'll experience the joy and satisfaction of finally knowing that sexual freedom lies not within the bounds of bedroom walls, but within ourselves!

Stress and Mental Health in Vietnam Veterans

The mental health problems of Vietnam veterans are unique in a number of ways. They've had to deal with the emotional trauma of participating not only in an unpopular war, but in a war that made them the brunt of hostility and criticism. As a result, many men still suffer from severe emotional damage from the war as well as from the psychological abuse they received when they finally returned home. Today, we look at Vietnam veterans differently than we have in the past; but thousands of veterans are still carrying the emotional scars of rejection. They need the benefits of social support groups in order to cope with the stress in their lives.

The emotional trauma of war doesn't end when one returns from battle. Wartime stress can be devastating and long-lasting for a young individual. Psychologists all agree that even emotionally stable individuals can develop serious war neuroses if exposed to sufficient stress. Stress related war disorders include flashbacks, nightmares, vivid memories of war, alienation, sleep disturbances, and exaggerated response to any kind of stimuli. In one study, more than 60 percent of the veterans interviewed still thought about death and dying and almost 70 percent reported having war-related nightmares. Many of these veterans continued to experience psychological stress 10 or more years after coming home from the war. In another study, it was found that Vietnam veterans, who were especially active in heavy combat situations, became more hostile and aggressive when they returned home and approved the use of violence more often than nonveterans did.

This pattern of psychological stress in veterans has also been seen in previous wars. When we look at past mental health records, we find that during World War II, as many as 500,000 individuals were discharged from the military because of psychological reasons. It's not even known how many of those veterans continued to have emotional problems. Or how many continue to have emotional problems even today.

When comparing the various types of coping strategies, it was found that positive social support had the biggest influence in helping veterans deal with post wartime stress. In some cases, intense psychiatric help is needed in order to alleviate severe stress disorders. In general, however, some of the most effective coping strategies are:

● Developing and mastering interpersonal relationships. This can be done by using behavior and attitude modification to improve one's outlook; learning communication skills to interact with others; and participating in outside activities to develop a social support network.

● Joining veterans groups and organizations. Groups that include people with similar experiences are a good way to cope with stress because you can "talk things out" with others who really know what you're going through.

● Using positive reinforcement strategies mentioned in previous chapters to improve self-image, raise low self-esteem, and condition the brain to respond in a positive and constructive way.

Coping With Stress Through Mutual Help Groups

For many of our problems, there are no easy answers or simple cures, but there are alternatives to coping alone. Mutual help groups can aid us in finding the hope and personal support we need because they offer us the most important outlet for recovery—the understanding and help of others who've gone through similar experiences.

Mutual help has been practiced since families first existed. As social beings, all of us need to be accepted, cared for, and emotionally supported. We also find it very satisfying to care for and support those around us. Within the most natural "mutual help networks—our families and friends—we establish the one-to-one contact so important to our happiness and well-being. This informal support is such a basic part of our social character that we're apt to take it for granted, but it clearly influences our ability to handle distressing events in our lives. Many of our daily conversations are actually mutual counseling sessions whereby we exchange the reassurances and advice that help us deal with routine stresses. In fact, research scientists have found that there's a strong link between the strength of our social support systems and our health.

The personal support we receive from family and friends, however, is only one part of the support network that helps sustain us through life. As we develop socially and intellectually, we tend to associate with others who have similar interests and beliefs. In groups such as religious congregations, civic and fraternal organizations, and social clubs, members benefit from a shared identity and a sense of common purpose. Through combined efforts, these groups can often promote or accomplish what the individual, acting alone, cannot. Our reasons for joining groups may vary considerably, but each member's presence and participation adds to the strength of the group. Thus, the group becomes an instrument for service to the total membership.

There's a special bond among people who share the same troubling experience; it begins when one person says to another, "I know just how you feel." Knowing that someone else truly understands one's feelings by virtue of having "been there" brings a sense of relief. The pain is no longer a solo burden. Stepping into the security of such a group of people can be like coming home for those of us who've been too long isolated by our private, painful experiences. Each mutual help group provides an atmosphere of acceptance that encourages the sharing of sorrows, fears, and frustrations. From there, we can begin to communicate more openly, view our problems more objectively, and find more effective coping strategies.

To those of us who are new to mutual help groups, being with others like ourselves, successfully getting on with life despite their problems, can be the best encouragement of all. While there are no levels of distinction among the members in a group, there are always those who are stronger, more experienced, more committed to the group's goals, and more able to give of themselves. These "helpers" often assume leadership roles and continue to receive comfort and encouragement while helping others. There's a natural tendency among those who have derived benefit from the group to want to perpetuate the cycle of being helped and helping. For those helpers who lead, organize, reach out to others, and bolster the group's morale by their own example—reward comes in seeing the progress of others. Says one group member, "I've been there and know what it's like. I could have been saved twenty years of misery if there had been a group to help me."

People are now taking a more realistic look not only at the formal care system, such as physicians and therapists, but at their own responsibility for self-care. Mutual help groups use the knowledge gained from a conflict or crisis as a valuable tool for building better ways to manage it. Some mutual help groups avoid formal professional guidance or consultation, although many have benefited from the informal help of professionals. And despite the distance maintained between the groups and their professional counterparts, each recognizes the role of the other; groups encourage their members to seek or continue with the professional help they need, and many physicians and other service providers actively endorse group programs as an appropriate extension of care. The most important thing to realize is that mutual help groups are there—to be joined, organized, or explored for better understanding. They're economical and effective. And, most importantly, they can reassure us that we're not alone. There are others who do understand and are anxious to share their experience and support with us.

There are a number of ways to get information about mutual help groups. Some of the larger ones are listed by subject in the phone directory, and the names and phone numbers of many more are available from hospitals and local mental health and social-service agencies. Directories of mutual help groups can usually be found in public libraries. As an introduction, I've listed some of the more common mutual help groups in the back of the book.

During the last few decades, a clear link has been established between negative life stress and mental health. An increase in negative events is associated with a worsening of symptoms, whereas a decrease in negative events is associated with an improvement in overall mental health. And even though many emotional disorders are not caused by stress, it now seems that a large number of mental problems, once thought to be unrelated to stress, have their roots in disturbing life events and experiences.

Throughout this chapter, one coping strategy stands out more than any other and that is the idea of developing social support systems and becoming involved with other people. No other stress therapy has had so much impact on so many different emotional problems. As a society-oriented people, we need other people to relate to and to communicate with. Without this part of our existence, most of us would be unable to deal with the mounting stresses that we're constantly subjected to at work and at home. This strong desire to be part of a group was recognized in a 17th century poem by John Donne who realized how important it is for people to be involved with one another.

> *No man is an island entire of itself*
> *Everyman is a piece of the continent, a part of the main*
> *Any man's death diminishes me, for I am involved in mankind*
> *And therefore never send to know for whom the bell tolls;*
> *It tolls for thee*

We can't be individual islands and expect to survive emotionally in a society that places such a premium on social support. When we deny ourselves the opportunity to interrelate with others, we're diminished because we don't allow ourselves to be involved with humankind. We're all part of the main—society in general and our community in particular. Unless we take advantage of our strong human need to have relationships with other people and become involved with one another, we'll continue to have high rates of stress-induced adult and childhood disease, mental health problems, and suicide. In our stress-filled society, we all have a stake in each other's lives, because when that bell tolls for one of us, it's really tolling for all of us.

7

Stress and Aging

All living organisms undergo a process of "senescence" in which cells begin to die and bodily functions gradually deteriorate. No one has been able to determine exactly how our body ages or why we're genetically programmed to live only a certain amount of time. We do know that biological aging involves a progressive decline or loss of nerve transmission, metabolism, rate of blood flow, respiratory capacity, resistance to infection, and ability to repair genetic material (DNA). As aging continues, our body is increasingly less likely to respond positively to challenges and more likely to be affected by negative events and situations.

During the later part of our life span, cells throughout our body degenerate and begin to die off more quickly than ever before. Factors that influence or speed up this cell degeneration and death are diet, toxic chemicals, amount of exercise, and general physical and emotional stress. Thus, both external and internal factors can contribute to longevity and greatly influence the overall rate of the aging process.

Aging, besides being a physically stressful process, is a very emotionally stressful time of life. It isn't unusual to experience some kind of mental health problem as we grow older. The aging or aged individual is more susceptible to mental illness and more prone to the effects of stress due to several factors.

1. Aging causes a decrease in the immune system's ability to attack foreign bodies. Therefore, stress makes the elderly more susceptible to illness and disease. Being ill more often than ever before is a real trauma that often leads to emotional disorders.

2. Increased illness and disease, together with the stress of aging itself, causes additional emotional stress and leads to even greater conditioned stress responses. This negative condition-

ing has the effect of making the elderly more and more prone to stress disorders.

3. The cumulative effect of years of stress responses begins to take its toll. The more stress episodes the body has had to respond to, the greater the damage will eventually be.

Older people are likely to experience two kinds of stresses: those that are "normal" to aging and those that are imposed by the environment. For younger populations, major illnesses, personal losses, and other extraordinary crises generally take place one at a time. In contrast, the aging phase of life is often characterized by the relative abruptness, clustering, and interaction of age-related problems. The stresses of illness, personal loss, diminished income, retirement, inadequate housing, etc. interact with social stresses such as prejudice and noncaring to produce isolation, loneliness, and depression. The cumulative effect of multiple stresses is typical for older people and is one of the major factors in triggering stress-related illness.

During this century, both life expectancy and the number of individuals 65 years of age and older have been increasing steadily (figures 7a and 7b). As a result, older people are playing a much greater role in government, economics, cultural and social activities, and in the work force. But even though they're becoming a greater portion of the population, they're also having to adjust to a society that's quick to recognize youth and new ideas yet slow to recognize age as a vital, experienced, and functional part of that society. The problems of aging include not only physical and mental health, but the emotional stress of being separated from the rest of the population. In this chapter, I'll discuss the aging process and how stress affects our ability to cope with it in a positive way. I'll also discuss strategies for dealing with various aging problems and what we can do to alleviate some of the stress we encounter as we grow older.

Stress Hormones and Aging

The "stress hormones," discussed in chapter one, are so called because they're released during stress and help our body defend itself against negative stress reactions. As we age, these stress hormones begin to act on our body in different ways and they make our response to stress more acute and much more damaging. When

Year	Life Expectancy (years)
1920	54.1
1930	59.7
1940	62.9
1950	69.7
1960	69.7
1970	70.9
1980	73.7
1983	74.7

Figure 7a
Life expectancy of the U.S. population from 1920 to 1983.
From Statistical Abstracts of the United States, 1985.

Year	No. Individuals (millions)	% of total population
1960	16.5	9.2
1970	19.5	9.6
1980	25.7	11.3
1985	28.6	11.8
Projected 1990 to 2080		
1990	31.7	12.8
2000	34.9	13.1
2030	64.6	21.3
2080	73.1	23.5

Figure 7b
Number and percent of total population of individuals 65 years
and older in the United States. From Statistical Abstracts of the
United States, 1985 and U.S. Bureau of the Census, Current
Population Reports, Series P-25 No's 949 and 952.

released, stress hormones interact with the normal aging processes and gradually create a climate that can speed up cell death, disease formation, and the loss of general bodily functions. In essence, while stress hormones are important for survival, they may actually contribute to the acceleration of aging.

Another important aspect of aging is the possibility that "brain aging" may act as a pacemaker or trigger for other forms of aging because of changes in the way these hormones regulate the central nervous system. Research done by Dr. Philip Landfield of the Bowman Gray School of Medicine suggests that stress hormones may be responsible for some of the gradual changes that take place within the brain during aging. Over the past several years, Dr. Landfield has found that the blood levels of stress hormones in experimental animals correlate significantly with the degree of age-related changes in the brain. He also observed the acceleration of structural changes in the brain like those of aging during long-term administration of stress hormones to experimental animals. Most recently, he has found that when rats have their source of stress hormones—their adrenal glands—surgically removed, they show fewer signs of brain aging than do other rats of the same age.

In a related study, Dr. Bernard Wexler of the Jewish Hospital in Cincinnati suggests that the tempo of modern living, as well as physical stress, can alter internal body chemistry and lead to premature blood vessel disease and aging. His results show that the overactivity of glands that regulate hormone responses to stress may lead to illnesses and diseases found in aged individuals. He says that, despite the great increase in life expectancy, the ever intensified demands of modern living may actually be contributing to accelerated aging. These and many other studies demonstrate that biological aging is somehow altered as a result of long-term exposure to stress hormones. As we age, we need to be even more aware of stress and stress reactions as major factors in aging and disease.

Psychological Stress of Aging

Unlike biological aging, which is the result of basic genetic and physical mechanisms, psychological aging depends on a lifetime of experiences. These experiences condition us to perceive events in certain ways and to respond to those events in our own particular manner. And while biological aging involves the death of cells and deterioration of bodily functions, psychological aging involves the death of positive attitudes and behaviors. The death of positive attitudes and behaviors is what causes us to experience severe stress reactions and what makes us susceptible to serious and debilitating mental health problems as we age.

When a survey was taken by the National Council on Aging, there was a great discrepancy between what younger people thought about the elderly and what the elderly initially thought about themselves. According to the survey, older people, who are just beginning to reach retirement age, report having positive self-images, being able to adapt well to changes, and being a valuable part of society. Several years after retirement, however, there's a general tendency for those positive self-images to decline. The difference between how older people then think of themselves and how younger members of our society think of them leads to "self-fulfilling prophecies" in which negative beliefs about aging cause lowered expectations, negative attitudes, and poor self-images. This causes older individuals to doubt their own worth and to perceive aging through the eyes of younger people. When that happens, they take on a distorted view of themselves and become more despondent and prone to stress effects. The fear, depression, and anxiety of growing old in this kind of environment invariably leads to tremendous emotional strain which magnifies and intensifies the stress response.

At the present time, there's no evidence at all that aging produces a change in intelligence, learning capacity, memory, or information processing. In fact, while some special skills aren't performed so successfully after 40, intellectual functions that rely on the application of learned material remains intact well into our 70's.

This was clearly demonstrated in a 21-year study conducted at the University of Southern California's gerontology research institute. The study showed that subjects, ranging from the age of 22 to 81 years of age, all maintained their levels of intellectual competence—or actually improved—as they grew older. Even between the ages of 74 and 81, about ten percent of the subjects tested performed better intellectually over the 21 year period than they had at younger ages!

In another study, done at the University of Rochester, researchers found that aged brains had longer and more extensive nerve fibers in the cortex than did brains of younger individuals. Since nerve fibers in the cortex provide information to the area of the brain responsible for learning and memory, it seems that the capacity for processing information can go on despite age. The point at which brain nerve degeneration begins to overtake nerve growth hasn't been determined yet since the oldest brain studied was 92 years old and still had an extensive network of nerve fibers.

These and other aging studies have proven that intelligence doesn't peak at an early age and then declines as one grows older. Intelligence and the capacity to learn can be a lifelong ability and a good reason for older people to remain active and productive throughout their lives.

One of the greatest psychological stresses for older individuals is knowing that there's no change in their ability to learn and carry out mental tasks, yet there is widespread bias against them in society and in the workplace. This tremendous emotional distress causes depression, which is the most common mental disorder affecting aging individuals. In fact, nearly 50 percent of older people admitted to mental hospitals suffer from some degree of depression. One out of four suicides is committed by a person 60 years or older, and a large number of these result from depression. The psychological impact of aging creates this kind of severe stress response because, as we age, we allow our negative perceptions of aging to shape our behavior and attitudes. Successful aging can only be accomplished if we eliminate those negative perceptions and learn to cope with the stresses of age in a vibrant and positive way.

Aging, Personality, and Mental Health

As we age, our mental health really depends on how successfully we adapt to life events as well as on our own personality type. According to one group of age researchers, personality is the pivotal factor in predicting which individuals will age successfully (i.e. with good physical and mental health). This is because personality is a key element in our ability to come to terms with our life experiences and situations. The individual most likely to age successfully is one who's able to reach high life satisfaction through his or her ability to interact with others and to become involved in outside activities. In other words, the person who can find and utilize support systems and other effective avenues of coping. Regardless of how old we are, most of us can't seem to cope well by ourselves and, therefore, we need to seek out support networks and various outside activities in order to help us minimize the stress of aging.

Outside activities are an excellent way to replace losses such as the loss of a spouse, a job, health, and recognition. Very often, the difference between successful and unsuccessful aging is our willingness to accept loss and a desire to adapt to changes and challenges. In order to help the adaptation process, older individuals need to maintain physical activity, social interaction, emotionally and intellectually stimulating activities, and self-care capabilities. Without these, there's social isolation, physical disability, frustration, and apathy. These, in turn, can quickly lead to depression, anxiety, and other mental illnesses.

The Life Satisfaction Index: How Successfully Are You Aging?

Here are some statements about life in general that older people feel differently about. Read each statement carefully, and if you agree with it, put a check mark in the space under "AGREE." If you don't agree with a statement, put a check mark in the space under "DISAGREE." If you're not sure one way or the other, leave the spaces blank. At the end of the list of statements is a scoring key which should give you an idea of how successful you really are at aging well.

AGREE DISAGREE

1. As I grow older, things seem better than I thought they would be.

2. I've gotten more of the breaks in life than most people I know.

3. This is the dreariest time of my life.

4. I'm just as happy as when I was younger.

5. My life could be happier than it is now.

6. These are the best years of my life.

7. Most of the things I do are boring or monotonous.

8. I expect some interesting and pleasant things to happen to me in the future.

9. The things I do are as interesting   _____ _____
    to me as they ever were.

10. I feel old and somewhat tired.   _____ _____

11. I feel my age, but it doesn't   _____ _____
    bother me.

12. As I look back on my life, I'm   _____ _____
    fairly well satisfied.

13. I wouldn't change my past life   _____ _____
    even if I could.

14. Compared to other people my age,   _____ _____
    I've made a lot of foolish decisions in my life.

15. Compared to other people my age,   _____ _____
    I make a good appearance.

16. I've made plans for things I'll   _____ _____
    be doing a month or a year from now.

17. When I think back over my life, I   _____ _____
    didn't get most of the important
    things I wanted.

18. Compared to other people, I get   _____ _____
    down in the dumps too often.

19. I've gotten pretty much what I   _____ _____
    expected out of life.

20. In spite of what people say, for   _____ _____
    most of us, things are getting
    worse, not better.

21. I think about my age so much that I _____ _____
    can't sleep.

22. I get angry more often than I used to. _____ _____

23. I have as much pep as I did last year. _____ _____

24. I see enough of my friends and   _____ _____
    relatives.

25. Many times, I feel that life isn't   _____ _____
    worth living.

26. Life is hard much of the time.   _____ _____

27. I'm not afraid of very many things   _____ _____
    now that I'm older.

28. As I get older, I feel less useful.   _____ _____

29. Compared to other people my age,   _____ _____
    I keep pretty active.

30. I don't usually feel lonely.   _____ _____

Score one point for each response that indicates life satisfaction. The appropriate life satisfaction responses for each statement are:

1.	Agree	16.	Agree
2.	Agree	17.	Disagree
3.	Disagree	18.	Disagree
4.	Agree	19.	Agree
5.	Disagree	20.	Disagree
6.	Agree	21.	Disagree
7.	Disagree	22.	Disagree
8.	Agree	23.	Agree
9.	Agree	24.	Agree
10.	Disagree	25.	Disagree
11.	Agree	26.	Disagree
12.	Agree	27.	Agree
13.	Agree	28.	Disagree
14.	Disagree	29.	Agree
15.	Agree	30.	Agree

Scoring key: 25–30 = High Life Satisfaction: You're aging very successfully because you don't let your age get in the way of enjoying life. You have positive attitudes and a good outlook that keep you young at heart.

15–24 = Average Life Satisfaction: You need to work on your attitudes and participate in more activities. There are times in your life when you could become more committed. Make sure that negative attitudes and behaviors don't begin to affect your health and well-being. Try to improve on those areas that you scored low on.

0–14 = Low Life Satisfaction: You're not aging successfully at all. You need to begin taking immediate steps to improve your overall mental attitude and start participating in activities. Your goal should be to join clubs, do volunteer work, or do anything else that will turn your life around. Becoming involved should be the first step in transforming your unsuccessful aging into successful aging.

Aging and Job Stress

Longer life expectancy, better pension plans, and decreased need for manual labor have all added to the problems of the older worker. But it's the physical changes such as reduced muscle strength, reduced mobility, and reduced capacity to work at high speed that make the older worker more susceptible to emotional stress. These traits are often seen as negative, even though studies show older people have a deeper sense of responsibility and loyalty, a great capacity for precision work, a low turnover and absenteeism rate, and are more experienced than younger people. Positive traits like these are often overlooked by managers and employers even though the advantages of having older workers far outweigh any disadvantages that may come up.

Fortunately, companies throughout the world, including many in the United States, are beginning to recognize the value of older workers. Stress management strategies used by these companies greatly reduce age-related stress because they help emphasize the positive aspects of age and give workers a sense of value and worth.

Among the measures companies can take to reduce stress and mental health problems in the older worker, three have proven to be very successful. These are:

1. Adjust work to accommodate the older worker. Since the older worker is so valuable in terms of experience, responsibility, and loyalty, it makes good sense to redesign certain jobs in order to keep a balance between work demand and decreased capacity. This may include adjustments in work hours, changes in work routines, shifting responsibilities, and improving work conditions such as lighting and climate. Anything a company can do to give older workers a feeling that they're needed will go a long way toward improving job satisfaction and productivity.

2. Recognize achievement through equitable job changes and rewards. As one ages, increasing importance is placed on prestige and on meaningful work. Social prestige is much more critical for the older worker than for the younger worker because of changing priorities and attitudes. Often, younger workers get the better jobs because they're the "future of the company" while older workers are relegated to less important and disproportionately lower paying jobs. Implementing fair and equitable job changes which emphasize the skills, experience, and knowledge of older workers is vital in maintaining a stress free workplace.

3. Improve health care services. With increasing age comes increasing need for health care. Providing good physical and mental health care opportunities will not only enhance performance, efficiency, and productivity of workers, but it will promote a stress free workplace because of improved worker morale.

In order to appreciate the advantages older workers have and to decrease stress caused by unfair work practices, managers and supervisors need to recognize the positive aspects of age in the workplace. As life spans increase and death rates decrease, the average age of the work force is becoming higher. Providing for the older worker by improving the overall work environment should be an important and worthwhile stress management goal for every company to meet.

Diet, Nutrition, and Aging

Some of the physical and psychological changes we experience as we grow older are believed to be influenced by the habits of a lifetime—the foods eaten, the amount of physical exercise, smoking, drinking, and drug taking. And almost all experts agree that nutrition is a factor in the aging process. Nutrition and stress are often linked during aging because older people begin to change eating habits as they become stressed more often. A cycle begins to occur in which stress leads to poor eating habits which lead to chronic illness which in turn leads to even greater stress.

As we get older, the rate at which our body uses energy tends to decrease. Food intake is lower, and the amount of lean body tissue decreases while the amount of body fat increases. These conditions tend to get worse during aging because eating habits are affected by stressful situations such as loneliness, depression, poor teeth, illness, income limitations, and increased alcohol and medicine use. Many older people compensate for taste loss by eating more highly seasoned foods, which can lead to salt or sugar overuse. Poor gums and teeth may make chewing more difficult, which results in diets limited to foods that are easy to chew but may be lacking in essential nutrients. These kinds of poor eating habits can certainly alter the blood levels of stress hormones, affect the biological aging process, and lead to many age-related illnesses and diseases.

As we age, we need to be more concerned about dietary needs and more careful about dietary products for which false nutritional claims are made. Unnecessary and ill-advised use of vitamin and mineral supplements can become excessive and lead to potentially toxic side effects. The ingestion of "megavitamins—large amounts of individual nutrients or combinations—concerns many scientists because large doses of some nutrients can have very damaging effects. An excess of vitamin A, for instance, can cause headaches, nausea, diarrhea, and eventual liver and bone damage. High doses of vitamin D can cause weight loss, weakness, excessive urination, bone deformities, and kidney damage. Excessive amounts of iron can build up to harmful levels in the liver and other body organs. Misconceptions about vitamins are not unusual. Here are four of the most common myths about them:

Myth #1:   Organic or natural vitamins are nutritionally superior to synthetic vitamins.

Fact #1:   Synthetic vitamins, manufactured in the laboratory, are identical to the natural vitamins found in foods. The body cannot tell the difference and gets the same benefits from either source. Statements like "Nature cannot be imitated" and "Natural vitamins have the essence of life" are totally without meaning.

Myth #2:   Vitamins give you "pep" and "energy."

Fact #2:   Vitamins yield no calories, they don't provide energy, and they don't construct any part of the body. They're needed for transforming the foods we eat into energy and body maintenance.

Myth #3:   The more vitamins the better.

Fact #3:   Taking excess vitamins is a complete waste, both in money and effect. In fact, too much of some vitamins can be very harmful.

Myth #4:   You cannot get enough vitamins from the conventional foods you eat.

Fact #4:   Anyone who eats a reasonably varied diet of whole food should normally never need supplemental vitamins.

Some supplements—like the misnamed "vitamin B15" (or "pangamic acid") —have proven to be valueless despite claims made for them. Pangamic acid is sometimes promoted as a treatment for heart disease, diabetes, glaucoma, allergies, and other ailments. Another unnecessary supplement sold in pill form is superoxide dismutase (SOD), sold as an "antiaging" pill. SOD has also proven to be useless in decreasing the aging process.

Virtually all nutrition experts agree that a well-balanced diet will provide most elderly people who are in good health with the nutrients they need for healthy living. A proper diet, the National Institute on Aging advises, should include:

- At least two servings of milk or other dairy products such as cheese, cottage cheese, or yogurt.
- Four servings of high-protein foods such as lean meat, poultry, fish, eggs, dried beans, nuts, or peanut butter.
- Four servings of fruits and vegetables, including citrus fruit or juice and a dark green leafy vegetable.
- Four servings of bread or cereal products made with whole grain or enriched flour, rice, or pasta.

Food and Drug Interactions

While food is essential for life, drugs are important too, when used to treat or prevent illness. Mixed together, however, foods and drugs can interact in ways that can diminish a drug's effectiveness or deprive the body of the nutrients it's receiving. Food can have both short and long-term effects on the way drugs behave in the body. It can speed up or slow down the absorption of a drug, influence the time it takes for the drug to pass through the gastrointestinal tract, and alter the way in which it's metabolized for use in the body. In some instances, certain food-drug combinations can produce serious illness, even death. When improper eating habits are combined with improper use of medications, the physical and mental reactions that often occur lead to severe emotional stress. Since stress has a tendency to make us change our eating habits and use of medication even more than usual, improper use of drugs and food creates an ongoing stress situation that makes us very prone to depression and other mental illnesses.

Although food and drug interactions can occur in people of all ages, they pose special problems for the elderly, who are major users of prescription and over-the-counter drugs. Studies show that more than half of the elderly are taking at least one medication a day. Many are taking six or more. What's more significant is that they're less likely than younger patients to be well-informed about how and when to take these drugs. Some take over-the-counter drugs, along with prescription drugs, without consulting their doctors and without considering that over-the-counter drugs can be just as hazardous. The accompanying side effects of taking multiple prescription and nonprescription drugs can lead to confusion and severe emotional stress because the body may react in a negative and often alarming way. The stress response, discussed in chapter one, can become so intense and the immune response so depressed that instead of helping fight an illness, multiple drug taking can actually make it worse! Add the wrong foods to all this and the combination can cause serious and sometimes fatal health problems. Older patients need to become more educated and informed about medications by challenging their physicians to explain what they're being given and to discuss the effects of food-drug interactions. Here are some of the most common food-drug interactions occurring in the elderly which can cause serious stress responses.

Drug	Food	Interaction
Tetracycline	Dairy products	Impairs drug absorption and increases infection
Anticoagulants	Liver, leafy green vegetables	Hinders anticlotting of blood
MAO inhibitors	Fermented foods, wines, beef and chicken livers, cola beverages, coffee, chocolate, raisins, bananas	Raises blood pressure to dangerous levels and can cause severe headaches
Hypertension medications	Licorice or licorice extracts	Neutralizes medication; aggravates hypertension

Alcohol can interact with many drugs, and when consumed in excess, plays havoc with our health. Intoxication can occur more rapidly when alcohol and certain medications are taken together. Consumed with tranquilizers, barbiturates, and antihistamines, alcohol can compound the depressant effects of those drugs on the central nervous system and slow down performance skills, judgment, and alertness. Alcohol can also cause other drugs—anticonvulsants and anticoagulants, for example—to be metabolized more rapidly, producing exaggerated responses. It can raise blood sugar levels and interfere with drugs prescribed for diabetes. With monoamine oxidase (MAO) inhibitors, which are prescribed for depression, alcohol or fermented foods can cause sharp increases in blood pressure, sometimes causing severe headaches, brain hemorrhage, even death in extreme cases. With diuretics, alcohol can reduce blood pressure, causing dizziness and accidents. With antibiotics, it can produce nausea, vomiting, headaches, and stomach cramps. Alcohol may also destroy the coating of time-released capsules, causing more rapid absorption of a drug into the system. All these things significantly increase the likelihood of succumbing to stress and stress reactions.

Certain drugs may also promote dietary deficiencies. Antacids contain aluminum hydroxide, which can contribute to phosphate deficiency. Aspirin, which is the drug of choice for treating arthritis, can cause small amounts of bleeding in the gastrointestinal tract which lead to iron depletion. A person taking lots of aspirin may need to follow a diet higher in iron. Some studies suggest that long-term aspirin users may also need diets high in folic acid and vitamin C.

Laxatives can also affect nutrient uptake. Some affect vitamin D absorption, which in turn can make a poor calcium balance even worse. Laxatives containing mercury can cause depletion of phosphorus from bones. And mineral oil, a widely used constipation remedy, can interfere with the absorption of vitamins A, D, E, and K and can also interfere with anticoagulants (given to prevent blood clotting).

What can we do to prevent undesirable food-drug interactions? Here are a few suggestions.

● Read the labels on over-the-counter remedies and the package inserts that come with prescription drugs.

● Follow your doctor's orders about when to take drugs and what foods or beverages to avoid while taking medications.

● Don't be afraid to ask how drugs might interact with your favorite edibles, especially if you consume large quantities of certain foods and beverages. While taking drugs, be sure to tell your doctor about any unusual symptoms that follow eating particular foods.

● Eat a nutritionally well-balanced diet from a wide variety of foods. Use of a needed drug, even on a long term basis, is less likely to cause depletion of vitamins and minerals if your overall nutritional status is good.

Clearly, there's much we need to know about medication. Yet, surveys show that older patients often are lacking information about the medicines prescribed for them. The elderly, who take three times as many medications as the population in general, should find out as much as possible about their medications, especially about proper use and side effects. If an older person is taking any more than three different drugs at the same time, there's a strong possibility that these drugs are interacting in some way to cause a problem which may be worse than the illness being treated. This is especially true if the drugs are being taken excessively or improperly. The best way for the elderly to begin taking on a greater responsibility for their own drug use is by asking themselves and their doctors the following questions:

☐ Does the drug make me feel worse than the illness itself? If so, do I discontinue its use and report any adverse reactions to my physician?

☐ Am I taking drugs only upon medical advice and under a physician's supervision, not on the "prescription" of relatives, friends and neighbors?

☐ Is my personality or physical condition being negatively altered when I add another drug to my usage?

☐ Can one drug be substituted for another so as to eliminate any adverse side effects?

☐ Am I taking the minimum possible dosage that's required?

☐ Am I using a few drugs well instead of many drugs that cause confusion and improper usage?

☐ Do I discontinue using a drug when it's no longer required? Is the drug I'm taking really necessary?

☐ Do I clean out my medicine chest regularly and discard any old medicines? Are all medicine bottles labeled in large, clear letters? Do I take medicines only after checking the labels carefully and, at night, only with a light turned on?

☐ Do I carry in my wallet information about drugs or other special treatment being used, as well as my physician's name and telephone number? Do I have a list of all drugs and dosages I'm taking to show my doctor or pharmacist if I ever need to?

The aim of any drug treatment is to cure illness, relieve symptoms, and improve overall bodily functions. When these aims are not met, as a result of or in spite of, drug use, we have to examine why. Because we respond differently to drugs during the course of our life span, we need to become more aware of drug reactions and accept the fact that, as we age, we become more sensitive than ever before to food-drug interactions. We need to take greater responsibility for knowing how medicines are affecting us and what we can do if these medicines begin to cause adverse reactions. As we grow older, becoming ill more often doesn't have to be a negative and stressful experience. We need to make sure that the treatment isn't either.

Quackery in the Stress and Aging Business

This year, the stress of aging will cause us to spend millions of dollars on products that do nothing for us. Some may even harm us. And we'll do it for the same reasons people have done it since ancient times . . . we want to believe in miracles and we want to find simple solutions and shortcuts to better health. When we don't achieve what we're after, we become despondent, depressed, and especially prone to the effects of stress reactions.

It's hard to resist. All of us, at one time or another, have seen or heard about a product—a new and exotic pill, device, or potion—that can easily solve our most serious problem. With this product, we're told, we can eat all we want and still lose weight; we can grow taller or build a better body; we can overcome age, baldness, arthritis, even cancer. It sounds too good to be true. It is. But we're tempted to try the product in spite of all we know about modern medical science, or perhaps because of it. After all, many treatments we take for granted today were once considered miracles. In order to tell the difference, we need to be able to separate facts from fantasy.

Not all advertisements for aging and health products are false. In fact, the vast majority aren't. So, just what is quackery? Simply put, quackery is the promotion of a medical remedy that doesn't work or hasn't been proven to work. In modern times, quackery is known as health fraud. But whether it's called quackery or health fraud, the result is the same—unfulfilled wishes, wasted dollars, endangered health.

Often, quack products are fairly easy to spot, like the magic pills you're supposed to take to stay forever young. But sometimes the products are vaguely based on some medical report that we may have heard about in the news. In general, when looking over ads for medicines and medical devices, we need to watch out for those that seem to promise too much too easily. Today's biggest targets for quackery are arthritis, fitness and diet, aging, and cancer.

Many people believe that advertising is screened by a government agency and, therefore, all claims about health products must be truthful. This isn't the case with most health care products, except for those drugs and medical devices that require premarket approval by the FDA. There's no federal, state, or local government agency that approves or verifies claims in advertisements before they're printed. Law enforcement authorities can take action only after the advertisements have appeared. In many cases, businesses that sell these products change addresses every few weeks or months in order to avoid being caught. Here are some guidelines that will help identify quackery.

● Beware of fantastic testimonials. Health fraud promotersare fond of using testimonials from "satisfied users" to promote their wares because they can't get ethical health professionals to sanction their products. Watch out for testimonials that report fantastic medical results, especially when no medical support for the claim is offered.

● Apply the "it-sounds-too-good-to-be-true" test to ads. In most cases, if it sounds too good to be true, it probably is. Don't be caught up by glamorous words, unrealistic promises, fancy pictures, and catchy expressions. A good advertising copywriter can make any product sound almost too good to pass up.

● Look for characteristics and statements commonly used in quackery such as:
   A quick and painless cure.

   A "special," "secret," "ancient," or "foreign" formula, available only through the mail from one supplier.

   A single product effective for a wide variety of ailments.

   A scientific "breakthrough" or "miracle cure" that has been held back or overlooked by the medical community.

Before buying a suspect product or treatment, find out more about it. Quacks have always been quick to exploit fads and current thinking. Today, they take advantage of the growing elderly population and capitalize on the notion that there's a quick and simple solution to almost any problem. To find out about a product, check with one or more of the following:

- Your doctor, pharmacist, or other health professional
- The Better Business Bureau
- Your local consumer office
- The Federal Trade Commission, Washington, D.C. 20580
- Your nearest office of the Food and Drug Administration

Coping Strategies for The Elderly

Physiologic events take place during aging which alter both our physical and mental state and increase the likelihood of our becoming more prone to stress effects. Because of this, elderly individuals have to recognize and deal with the stressors that they as a group are especially susceptible to. Stress management for the elderly, therefore, has to include coping strategies that deal specifically with things like loneliness, physical disability, rejection, and feelings of worthlessness. Emotional stresses such as these are so powerful that older people often find it impossible to live or cope in a society that looks at them in any kind of negative way. And unless something is done, the stress of aging can be one of the most destructive mental and physical processes we'll experience in our lives.

Because we're more prone to the effects of stress as we age, coping strategies are very important for continued health and well-being. Among the many stress management strategies available, social support is especially well suited to the older individual because it focuses on social and emotional needs.

There's no question that social conditions affect physical ability and independence and contribute enormously to the health of older people. Widowers and elderly, living in areas where there's no social organization for them, increase their chances of succumbing to illness and disease. On the other hand, older people belonging to religious groups or close ethnic groups are buffered against stress-related disease because they exist within a well integrated community. In essence, they have many social and community ties.

For some time, social isolation has been suspected of increasing the aging process. In one study, for example, it was found that people lacking social ties had three times the mortality rate over a ten year period than people having close social ties. Being involved in social and community affairs, giving and seeking advice, and other forms of assistance had an important effect on how older people perceived their own health status. Furthermore, having close friends and confidants had a strong tendency to relieve stress and influence both physical and mental health. In another study, it was shown that the stresses of retirement, death of a spouse, and decreased activity were lessened as a result of having supportive exchange with an intimate friend.

Social support networks, then, serve to bring us back from isolation into a social community that will respond to our needs and offer us an outlet for sharing, communicating, and interacting. Some of the best social support networks are religious organizations, retirement associations and clubs, volunteer and charity organizations, and community action groups. These kinds of support groups can enrich our lives by making us feel useful and needed and by giving us a sense of dignity. Aging, after all, doesn't necessarily mean an end to our challenges, but the beginning of a new phase of our lives in which we fulfill those challenges in a different but equally enthusiastic and satisfying way. Here are nine other coping strategies that can help older people deal with the stress in their lives and slow down the aging process by improving health and well-being.

1. Participate in "enrichment programs." Human needs go beyond survival, subsistence, and medical care. Enrichment programs have varied goals. Some aim at sheer enjoyment and companionship. Others offer an opportunity to pursue old or new interests, to maintain old roles or develop new ones, to learn, or to make contributions to others. All these activities and programs are a way to increase self-esteem and to do something valuable and worthwhile.

2. Participate in sporting activities and exercise. A key factor in maintaining morale and self-image is the satisfying and constructive use of leisure time. When the use of leisure time also involves sports activity and exercise, it becomes an important contributing factor to promoting physical health. Endurance exercises (such as cycling, walking, and swimming) are recommended, but only after a careful checkup by a physician. In general, there's a very strong relationship between good health and active living which carries over into one's retirement days. Exercise helps us boost our energy reserves and triggers the release of endorphins which help us cope with both physical and mental stress.

3. Obtain proper health care. Older people tend to view minor health problems as "normal" to aging and, thus, they fail to get adequate medical treatment. Minor health problems then lead to major health disorders which then create intense physical and emotional stress situations. It's also important to accept mental health problems just as you would any other health problem. Self-depreciation, loss of appetite, and insomnia (especially awakening in the early morning hours) may be symptoms of depression, not aging. Never assume that any kind of physical or mental illness is a normal byproduct of age.

4. Get a pet. One of the more interesting findings about stress and the aging individual has been that pets are one of the best therapeutic tools and actually help the elderly cope with severe stress, depression, and loneliness. Pets are good medicine because they satisfy needs such as caring and a desire to be loved and needed. According to experts, as older people withdraw from human affairs more, their nonhuman environment becomes even more important. Animals fulfill the human craving for emotional relationships and promote interactions and involvement.

    Studies have shown that talking to and stroking animals can decrease blood pressure and that owning a pet can improve the chances of surviving a heart attack. Because pets are willing to accept and return love unconditionally, the older person not only has a companion to share love with, he or she also has a steady source from which to receive love whenever stress, depression, or loneliness set in.

5. Improve eating habits to stay healthy, strong, and resistant to disease. Several research programs around the country have shown that eating right (consuming all the required nutrients; eliminating fatty foods; and cutting down on quantities) can have an antiaging effect on the body and cut down on stress-related health problems. Eating right doesn't always mean you'll necessarily live longer; it does mean you'll experience fewer stress reactions and live a lot better as you grow older.

6. Eliminate destructive habits such as smoking and excessive drinking. Smoking and alcohol consumption are bad enough at any age. For older people, they can be downright deadly. Nicotine and other tobacco ingredients speed up metabolism of

certain drugs. Alcohol causes changes in the liver that also speed up metabolism of drugs such as anticonvulsants, anticoagulants, and diabetes medications. These drugs become less effective because they don't stay in the body long enough. If alcohol abuse damages the liver, the drugs remain in the body too long and cause further damage. Smoking and alcohol abuse, then, can bring on physical health problems not only by their own actions but by their interactions with drugs. Adverse drug reactions lead to negative stress reactions which can encourage even more smoking and drinking. The best way to avoid this kind of "stress cycle" is to stop smoking altogether and eliminate or moderate alcohol use.

7. Exercise the brain. Many studies have shown that the brain doesn't usually age much when it remains active and that keeping the brain vitalized prevents loss of thinking ability. In order to slow brain aging, older people should maintain high levels of brain activity by reading, writing, playing musical instruments, taking up new hobbies, learning new things, participating in volunteer activities that require thought and mental organization, and taking classes on anything from art to zoology. One of the most tragic things that happens to us as we become older is that we tend to sit back and give up on everything. Some of the best writers, poets, painters, musicians, scientists, and scholars in the world are well past their 60s and still going strong because they prevent their brains from becoming stagnant. We need to follow that example and never allow age to get in the way of our ambitions, dreams, or goals. Whether we believe it or not, most of us have the potential for great accomplishment no matter how old we are.

8. Do everything in moderation. People who live to an old age and stay healthy and stress free eat right and tend to lead a simple lifestyle. They consume a diet high in fiber and carbohydrates and low in fats and proteins; they take in only 1800 calories a day compared with the average American diet of 3300 calories a day; they drink little and they don't smoke. They also continue to work or to keep active until their deaths; tend not to worry about their age; and have many friends and social support groups. In essence, these healthy older people have found that

aging doesn't have to be a stressful experience if they just take care of themselves in mind and body.

9.   Learn relaxation exercises. A study of 45 elderly people living in retirement homes showed that the ones who practiced relaxation exercises and techniques had significant increases in natural killer (NK) cell activity and significant decreases in antibodies to herpes simplex virus—both indications of enhanced immune activity. This study, and others like it, suggest that reducing stress through the practice of relaxation can boost the body's disease-fighting ability and help prevent stress-related illness. This is especially important for older people because they tend to be much more susceptible to age-related breakdown of the immune response. Anything that helps prevent illness and disease and makes us feel good about ourselves is an instant stress reliever.

The evidence that stress can indeed accelerate the aging process is only now beginning to accumulate. As more and more long-term studies are done, it's becoming clear that stress reactions, especially stress hormone reactions, contribute to the deterioration of body tissues, breakdown of immune function, susceptibility to illness and disease, and acceleration of age-related structural changes in the brain. It's also clear that stress-induced activities and habits such as poor eating, smoking, drinking, improper drug use, etc. also have a tremendous influence on the overall aging process.

As we get older we need to be more aware of stress responses and be wary not to treat them as just "normal aging symptoms." By using coping strategies, maintaining good health habits, eating properly, belonging to social support groups, and practicing relaxation exercises, we can actually slow down the aging process and live out our lives in the healthiest way possible. The idea, after all, is not to live long and die old, but to live long and die young.

PART II

RELAXATION TECHNIQUES AND EXERCISES

INTRODUCTION

In the first part of this book, we learned what happens to us during stress and how stress reactions bring about many kinds of illness and disease. We saw how stress sources can be identified and eliminated by recognizing and charting physical and emotional symptoms, behavior patterns, and attitudes. And we discovered how our own habits and perceptions shape those behavior patterns and attitudes through a conditioning process that can trigger spontaneous stress responses.

We know that stress isn't something we can touch or see. Rather, it's a physical response that we create within ourselves because of the way we choose to react to events and situations in our lives. The only way to overcome this kind of mental response is through a stress management strategy that not only helps us change our attitudes and behavior, but helps us bring our bodies back into a state of rest and balance through conscious relaxation.

In this part of the book, I'll explain and give examples of various relaxation exercises that are the mainstay of any stress management strategy. No amount of attitude or behavior modification can totally replace relaxation as an effective tool for relieving stress. Because the stress response is such a powerful physiologic reaction, we need an equally powerful physiologic reaction to counter that response. We call this counter reaction the "relaxation response."

It takes our brain only a few seconds to send signals to the rest of our body; it takes our body seconds to begin to react to those signals in either a negative or positive way. As a result, what we do during those first few seconds sets into motion the mechanisms of physical response. And it's here that we can change that response from a negative and destructive "stress response" to a positive and beneficial "relaxation response."

Just as we modify behavior and attitudes, evoking that relaxation response can become a simple technique through conditioning and habit formation. It's only because we've spent a lifetime conditioning ourselves in a negative way that we think of the stress response as the only normal response to stress in nature. The relaxation response is just as natural and equally as sensitive to conditioning and habit formation. Our goal is to develop our ability to evoke the relaxation response so that it becomes instantly and automatically available to us whenever we need.

The remainder of this book describes ways to do just that. Once practiced and learned, relaxation exercises can bring our body back to a state of relaxation within 60 seconds, after which we can continue to relax for as long as we choose. And as we begin to condition ourselves to relax, we must never underestimate the power our brain has to control the multitude of responses and reactions our body is capable of. Learning to harness that power and using it to eliminate stress reactions is the key element behind successful one-minute stress management.

8

Progressive Muscle Relaxation (PMR)

All the muscles in our body, to some degree, are in a constant state of tension. If they weren't, we wouldn't be able to stand erect or move about very effectively. The problem most of us face when we try to relieve that tension is that we don't know how to do it. We try to relax by taking walks, by watching television, by sitting down and reading, or by just lounging around. These so-called "recreational" activities are really not the "conscious relaxation" activities we need to do in order to bring about complete relaxation of both mind and body.

Conscious relaxation is necessary so that our mind and body can experience the sensation of total muscular rest, as well as mental refreshment. Sleep, which is rest for the purpose of rejuvenating the body, can't take the place of relaxation exercises because even sleep doesn't bring about the deeply relaxed state we need to be in for truly effective tension relief.

The principle behind relaxation training is that tension is incompatible with relaxation. In other words, we either do one or the other. Whenever we relax our mind and our body, we automatically exclude the tension that produces muscular tenseness. Therefore, relaxation exercises produce a feeling of well-being and rest by creating a relaxed state that actually inhibits anxiety and negative stress reactions.

The degree to which our muscles are relaxed can be controlled by practicing a special technique called "Progressive Muscle Relaxation" or PMR. In PMR, the objective is to induce deep muscular relaxation by gradually releasing tension from various parts of the body one part at a time.

There are three basic positions which facilitate any kind of relaxation exercise, including PMR. These are: (1) lying position (figure 8a); (2) prone position (figure 8b); and (3) semireclining position (figure 8c). The semireclining position is useful whenever we're at work or any other place where lying down isn't possible. Most beginners find that lying down is the most effective position because it's the one which evokes the relaxation response the fastest. After learning a relaxation technique, any position can be equally effective and satisfying.

Regardless of which position is used, comfort is absolutely critical. Pillows should be placed under the head, knees, and arms, as shown in figure 8a, or under the face, pelvis, and feet, as shown in figure 8b. In the semireclining position, the chair should be soft and comfortable and have cushioned arms. If necessary, the forearms should be supported by placing pillows on the chair arms. The feet also need to be supported either by a foot rest or a pillow. The head must be in a comfortable position and supported by a chair, cushion, or pillow. Unless the body is totally comfortable, relaxation will be possible but won't be as effective. Therefore, body position and comfort are the principle starting points to begin any relaxation exercise.

Some people have found that music is also a big factor in helping them relax because they can concentrate on the music and forget about other distractions. When listening to music, however, make sure that it's not too loud and never too harsh. Good music for relaxation is any type of soft, classical music by Handel (Largo, for example), Bach (Air on G String, for instance), Saint-Saens (The Swan, for example), or another favorite composition that's soothing, soft, and melodic.

After assuming a comfortable position, either sitting in a chair or lying down, take your shoes off, close your eyes and begin concentrating on your muscle groups one at a time starting with your toes first. Here's a sample of the kind of self-instruction you can use to produce a relaxed state. After using these instructions several times, you'll know them by heart and be able to use them automatically whenever you feel tense. You may even want to shorten the self-instructions after becoming adept at bringing on relaxation. As you begin to condition yourself to relax, you'll notice that relaxation will come more quickly and with much less effort each time. With enough practice, you'll be able to relax your entire body within a minute of starting an exercise.

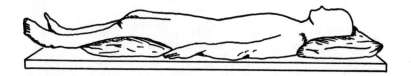

Figure 8a
Lying

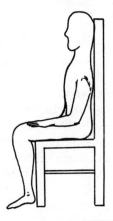

Figure 8b
Prone

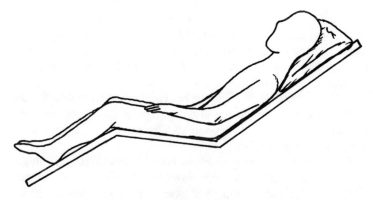

Figure 8c
Semireclining

PMR Self-Instructions

I'm falling into a nice, relaxed state; I'm breathing deeply, slowly, and smoothly . . . deeply, slowly, and smoothly. As I breathe, I'm becoming more and more relaxed . . . relaxed . . . relaxed. The toes on my feet are becoming numb; I feel a tingling sensation as the muscles in my toes become more relaxed and tension free . . . relaxed and tension free. They're getting more and more numb and heavy as I breathe. Each breath I take makes my toes become heavier and more numb . . . heavier and more numb. Now my toes are very heavy . . . very heavy. . . . very heavy. The heavy, numb sensation is making my toes feel totally relaxed . . . relaxed . . . relaxed . . . more relaxed with each breath I take.

The numbness is beginning to creep up from my toes to my feet. My feet are beginning to tingle as they get heavy and numb . . . heavy and numb. There's a slight burning sensation in my feet as if they were submerged in warm, refreshing water. As I breathe, I can feel my feet becoming more numb and more relaxed. The muscles in both feet are becoming loose and soft . . . loose and soft; they feel very warm, heavy and relaxed . . . relaxed . . . relaxed. . . . more relaxed with each breath I take. My feet are so warm and soft . . . warm and soft . . . relaxed . . . relaxed . . . relaxed. . . . more relaxed with each breath I take.

I feel the warmth and numbness going to my calves as I breathe and relax . . . breathe and relax. My calves are beginning to get very heavy and numb . . . heavy and numb. They're getting soft and warm as tension leaves and my muscles relax . . . relax . . . relax. With each breath I take, my calves are getting heavier and heavier . . . heavier and heavier, relaxed and numb, tension free and relaxed . . . relaxed . . . relaxed. . . . more relaxed with each breath I take. The warmth is soothing and refreshing . . . soothing and refreshing, relaxed . . . relaxed . . . relaxed. . . . more relaxed with each breath I take.

The numbness is going from my calves to my thighs. My thighs are now beginning to get warm and soft . . . warm and soft . . . loose and relaxed . . . loose and relaxed. My thighs are getting numb and heavy . . . numb and heavy; there's a tingling sensation as they become more numb and heavy . . . soft and relaxed . . . soft and relaxed. With each breath I take, my thighs are getting heavier . . . heavier . . . heavier. I feel the warmth and numbness creeping up my thighs and releasing tension. With each breath I take, my thighs feel more and more relaxed . . . relaxed . . . relaxed. . . . more relaxed with each breath I take.

My fingers are beginning to tingle and get numb as the warmth creeps into them. They're becoming soft and loose . . . soft and loose, warm and numb . . . numb . . . numb. I sense a numbness going from the tips of my fingers into my knuckles as I breathe slowly and relax . . . relax . . . relax. The warmth and numbness is going into my wrists and my wrists are getting warmer and warmer, softer and softer. My hands are heavy and relaxed . . . heavy and relaxed. With each breath I take my hands are heavy and relaxed . . . relaxed . . . relaxed. . . . more relaxed with each breath I take.

My arms are now beginning to get numb. The warmth is going from my hands into my arms and I feel heaviness and warmth . . . heaviness and warmth. As I breathe, my arms are getting heavier and heavier, numb and relaxed . . . numb and relaxed. A tingling and numbing sensation is going up my arms and releasing tension; my muscles are beginning to relax . . . relax . . . relax. My arms are very heavy now and relaxed . . . relaxed . . . relaxed . . . more relaxed with each breath I take.

The numbness in my arms is going into my shoulders. My shoulders are getting heavy and numb . . . heavy and numb. I can feel the warmth and heaviness loosening the muscles in my shoulders and they're getting more relaxed . . . relaxed . . . relaxed . . . more relaxed with each breath I take. As I breathe, tension is leaving my shoulders. They now feel very warm and numb . . . warm and numb, heavy and relaxed . . . relaxed . . . relaxed. . . . more relaxed with each breath I take.

Warmth is spreading from my shoulders into my chest. My chest feels warmer and warmer . . . looser and looser. With each breath I take, my chest is becoming heavy and numb . . . heavy and numb, soft and relaxed . . . relaxed . . . relaxed. I can feel the muscles in my chest tingle and become numb and heavy . . . numb and heavy. As I breathe, tension is leaving and my chest is relaxed . . . relaxed . . . relaxed. . . . more relaxed with each breath I take. My chest feels very heavy and numb now. With each

breath   I   take,   my   chest   is
relaxed . . . relaxed . . . relaxed . . . relaxed.

The numbness and warmth are traveling from my chest to my neck. My neck is becoming warm and numb . . . warm and numb. I can feel the tingling, numbing feeling in my neck as I breathe and relax . . . relax . . . relax . . . relax. My neck is getting heavier and heavier . . . warmer and warmer . . . more relaxed with each breath I take. The tension is leaving the muscles in my neck and my neck is relaxed . . . relaxed . . . relaxed. . . . more relaxed with each breath I take.

My face is getting softer and softer . . . softer and softer. The warmth is spreading from my neck into my face and it's getting warmer . . . warmer . . . warmer. As I breathe, my face is becoming heavier and heavier . . . relaxed and tension free. I feel all the tension leaving my facial muscles and they're becoming relaxed . . . relaxed . . . relaxed. . . . more relaxed with each breath I take.

My body feels warm and relaxed . . . relaxed . . . relaxed; heavy and numb . . . heavy and numb. My body is so heavy and relaxed that it's sinking into the chair. Tension is melting away; my body muscles are soft and relaxed . . . soft and relaxed, heavy and limp . . . heavy and limp. As I breathe, I feel a soothing warmth and I'm relaxed . . . relaxed . . . relaxed. Tension is flowing away;   With   each   breath   I   take,   I   can
relax . . . relax. . . . relax. . . . relax. . . . relax. . . . relax.

This is only a sample of the kind of self-instruction you can use. You may use anything that comes to your mind, providing it elicits a pattern of gradual relaxation throughout your body. You can also continue and prolong the instructions so that you set your own pace and bring about relaxation in your own way. When using PMR, however, there are several things you should remember in order to enhance the technique. These are:

1. Always make comfort the starting point of relaxation. Remove your shoes and tight-fitting clothing, loosen your belt, and take off any jewelry that's going to distract you when you come to that particular body part. Don't try to practice relaxation in a room that's too cold or too hot. Remember, anything that can distract you probably will.

2. Speak to yourself in a slow, rhythmic, and monotonous manner. This helps get you into a steady pace which facilitates relaxation.

3. Breathe slowly and rhythmically. It's important to use diaphragmatic breathing so that your breathing motion is smooth and uninterrupted. To make sure you're breathing properly, try this exercise. Place your right hand on your upper abdomen just above your navel and your left hand in the middle of your upper chest just above your nipples. When you breathe, the right hand should rise as you inhale and fall as you exhale; the left hand shouldn't move at all. After a few practice sessions, you should be able to breathe this way while having your hands at your sides in a relaxed state.

   Don't exhale all your breath at the beginning of each breath cycle. Make sure that each breath is long and even, smooth and gentle. This rhythmic smoothness allows our autonomic nervous system to take over and keep us relaxed and tension free. When giving repeated self-instructions such as relax . . . relax . . . relax . . . say each word slowly at the same speed and smoothness as your exhaling breath.

4. Use "soft" words like relax, soothing, smooth, heavy, limp, numb, etc. Avoid words that are harsh and make you feel tense or lose concentration.

5. Don't go on to the next body part until the part you're working on is relaxed.

6. When your body is completely relaxed, allow yourself to remain that way for several minutes before getting up to stretch.

Progressive muscle relaxation has been very effective in relieving a variety of stress-related illnesses such as hypertension, migraine headaches, and ulcers. But even if we don't suffer from these kinds of illnesses, it may be necessary to use this technique several times a day if we're in severe stress situations. After a short while, relaxation will become much easier and almost spontaneous. We'll have conditioned ourselves to bring on the relaxation response just as we would any other natural, physiologic reaction. Once we learn how our muscles should feel when they're relaxed, it becomes a matter of habit and conditioning to bring them into that relaxed state whenever we want to. When we can do that, taking part in challenging and exciting activities will become much more enjoyable because we'll never have to fear the threat of muscle tension again.

4. Breathe slowly and rhythmically. It's important to use an appropriate control so that you're breathing in a regular, smooth rhythm and not gasping. To make sure you're breathing correctly, try this exercise. Place your right hand in your upper abdomen just above your navel and your left hand in the middle of your upper chest just above your nipples. When you breathe, the right hand should rise as you inhale and fall as you exhale, and the left hand shouldn't move at all. After a few practice sessions, you should be able to breathe this way while leaving your hands at your sides in a relaxed state.
Don't capture all your breath when tensing, and [illegible] breathing cycle. Make sure that each breath is long and even, smooth and gentle. This rhythmic, smooth breathing allows the parasympathetic nervous system to take over and keeps you centered and calm. [illegible] relaxation [illegible] one [illegible] the [illegible] spoke [illegible] relaxing [illegible].

Use key words like relax, soothing, smooth, heavy, warm, numb, and other words that are linked to your own relaxation response.

5. Don't [illegible] practicing [illegible].

6. [illegible] your [illegible] relaxation [illegible] to [illegible] up to [illegible].

Progressive muscle relaxation has been very [illegible] personal [illegible] and [illegible] However [illegible] suffer from these kinds of illnesses [illegible] learn [illegible] relaxation, will become much easier and almost spontaneous. We'll have conditioned our [illegible] on the relaxation response [illegible] and our parasympathetic nervous system. Once we [illegible] our muscles should feel [illegible] they've [illegible] comfort and [illegible] relaxation [illegible]. When [illegible] because we'll never have to [illegible].

9

Tension-Relaxation

At first, some of us may have a difficult time learning exactly how relaxed muscles should feel because we rarely have a point of reference to judge tension by. The technique of tension-relaxation, developed by Dr. Edmund Jacobson, a Chicago physician, teaches us how to tell the difference. This simple and easily learned procedure consists of conscious muscular tension followed immediately by relaxation. The reason for alternating tension and relaxation is to become acutely aware of the differences between the tension and relaxation states.

The principle behind tension-relaxation is if we're not well attuned to what relaxation should feel like compared to tension, we won't be able to tell how effectively we're relaxing at any given time. When we try to relax without knowing the feeling of relaxation, our body won't be able to respond because our brain won't recognize tension as the stimulus it should be responding to. Tension-relaxation teaches us to discriminate between the two so that our brain can immediately sense when and where tension occurs and to react to it in a natural and spontaneous way.

The positions for the tension-relaxation technique are the same as those used for Progressive Muscle Relaxation. It's also important to be as comfortable as possible and not have any distractions or disturbances during the exercises. After practicing this technique daily for several weeks, the conditioning process will take over and our response will become easier and more automatic. Habits form that enable our muscles to relax at will regardless of the position we assume. The key element in shaping this conditioned response is our brain's innate ability to recognize degrees of physical tenseness and then to respond to that tenseness by relaxing the muscles almost involuntarily.

When first starting tension-relaxation exercises, different muscle groups are tensed individually during separate exercise sessions.

These are: hands, arms, legs, chest, back, shoulders, neck, and forehead. Only after the individual muscle groups are mastered should you put the technique all together and use it to relax all the muscle groups in one session. By practicing the technique for each separate body region, the conditioning process is much more effective and total body relaxation will become much easier. Later, some of the muscle groups, such as hands and arms, shoulders and neck, can be combined so that relaxation is achieved by concentrating on only a few muscle groups.

Eventually, the tension part of tension-relaxation can be eliminated altogether because relaxation will become a classically conditioned response. You'll be able to relax your entire body at once or only the specific parts of your body that are especially tensed. A word of caution, however. Always be aware of your ability to recognize tension versus relaxation. That ability is the cornerstone of tension management and should always be your principle focus when trying to relieve tension in any part of your body. If you begin to have trouble doing that, go back to tension as a means of reconditioning yourself to again recognize the difference between the two muscle states.

The following are eight sets of tension-relaxation exercises, one for each muscle group. As you perform each exercise set, you should carry out the movement to its absolute limit before slacking off the muscle completely and resting. After reaching maximum contraction, stay tensed for at least ten seconds in order to get the full impact of what it feels like to become relaxed. Remember, the more tension you place on each muscle group, the greater the subsequent feeling of relaxation will be.

Practice Session #1—Hands

Tension: With hands at your sides, clench your fists as hard as possible. Keep them clenched for at least ten seconds. At first, you may want to tense only one hand at a time.

Relaxation: Release your hands and let your fingers slowly uncurl and go limp at your sides.

Note: Repeat this exercise three times, remembering to keep extending for at least ten seconds after maximum tension. After three sets, keep your hands and body relaxed and rested for twenty to thirty minutes.

Practice Session #2—Arms

Tension: Raise your arms and clench your fists very tightly for at least ten seconds. At first, you may want to tense only one arm at a time.

Relaxation: Allow your arms to fall limply to your sides. Your fingers should hang loosely and motionless.

Note: Repeat this exercise three times with maximum tension each time. After three sets, keep your arms very still and limp for twenty to thirty minutes.

Practice Session #3—Legs

Tension: Push your feet downward as far and as hard as you can for at least ten seconds. The toes of each foot should also be bent down at the same time.

Relaxation: Allow your feet and toes to go limp and to relax with your legs being very loose.

Note: Repeat this exercise three times with maximum tension each time. After three sets, keep your legs very still and limp for twenty to thirty minutes. Never cross your legs while doing this exercise.

Practice Session #4—Abdomen

Tension: Pull in your abdominal muscles as much as you can. Keep them pulled in for at least ten seconds.

Relaxation: Slowly release your abdominal muscles and lie perfectly still.

Note: Repeat this exercise three times with maximum pulling each time. Breath slowly and allow your abdomen to relax. After three sets, remain rested for twenty to thirty minutes.

Practice Session #5—Back

Tension: Arch your spine upward as far as you can until only your head and buttocks are touching the floor or bed. Keep your back arched maximally for at least ten seconds.

Relaxation: Gradually lower your back and let it become heavy and loose.

Note: Repeat this exercise three times. If necessary, place a small pillow underneath your lower back for more comfort. Remain relaxed for twenty to thirty minutes. This particular exercise is best done only in a fully reclined position.

Practice Session #6—Shoulders

Tension: Shrug your shoulders toward your head as hard as you can for a full ten seconds.

Relaxation: Release and lower your shoulders slowly. Let them rest limply and heavily.

Note: Repeat this exercise three times with maximum tension each time. After three sets, relax your shoulders and lie quietly for twenty to thirty minutes.

Practice Session #7—Neck

Tension: Push your head backward against a pillow or mattress as hard as you can for a full ten seconds.

Relaxation: Release your head and let it lie quiet and motionless.

Note: Repeat this exercise three times. Instead of pushing your head backward, you can also lift it forward as far as it will go for a full ten seconds before letting it drop back down to relax. After three sets, let your head remain relaxed for twenty to thirty minutes.

Practice Session # 8—Forehead

Tension: Wrinkle your forehead as much as you can and hold it wrinkled for a full ten seconds.

Relaxation: Slowly release the forehead muscles and let your face relax completely.

Note: Repeat this exercise three times. It may be easier to tense the forehead muscles by frowning severely rather than wrinkling. You can also try to alternate wrinkling and frowning. After three sets, keep your face and head relaxed for twenty to thirty minutes.

When using tension-relaxation techniques, we need to follow certain rules and guidelines in order to make relaxation more effective and easier to learn. These are:

1. Try to set aside a specific time every day to practice, even if it's only a few minutes each day. The best times to practice are in the evening after a full day of tension or in the morning to help you get relaxed for the start of a day. However, be careful not to do exercises right before going to bed. If you wait until you're too tired, your mind won't be in the proper state to practice and the natural conditioning process won't be as effective.

2. Always wear loose, comfortable clothing when practicing relaxation techniques. Remove your shoes, loosen your buttons, and make sure you don't have anything around your neck. Also, remove jewelry such as watches and necklaces in order to prevent small distractions from ruining your practice session. Keep your eyes closed during the entire practice session and never cross your arms or your legs.

3. Try not to practice on a full stomach. During digestion, more circulating blood than normal is diverted to the gastrointestinal tract and away from muscles and other tissues. Lowered blood levels in muscles may cause cramps and discomfort during tension. Also, a full stomach will make you feel sluggish and keep you from concentrating as well as you should on the exercises.

4. Make sure you practice in a room that's quiet, well ventilated, not too well lit, and not too hot or cold. Any physical distraction will decrease the effectiveness of the exercises.

5. Muscles should always be relaxed slowly and gradually after tension, never abruptly. This will give you a better feeling of the transition between complete tension and complete relaxation. Let your body movements be smooth and gentle, always flowing with your breath. During tension, never hold your breath—just let it flow naturally.

6. During each practice session, try to relax the muscle groups that you've previously worked on. For example, during practice session 3, while relaxing your legs, also relax your hands and arms. After the eighth practice session, you should be able to relax all the muscle groups each time you tense and relax individual muscle groups.

7. After muscles groups are tensed and relaxed, it may help you to actually visualize them becoming loose and limp—this is called "imaging." With smooth, rhythmic breathing, imagine your muscles becoming heavier and heavier. See them getting soft and tender. Give special attention to those muscle groups that are particularly difficult to relax completely. Most importantly, don't give up. Some days may be worse than others and it's vital to repeat the tension-relaxation exercises daily at first so that relaxation becomes second nature.

Tension-relaxation is one of the best and most effective ways to learn relaxation because it conditions us to immediately distinguish between tensed and relaxed muscles. In other words, we actually acquire an ability to recognize even small degrees of tension within each individual muscle group. Dr. Edmund Jacobson has termed the innate ability to recognize tension as the "cultivation of muscle sense." Cultivating this muscle sense can only be accomplished if we condition our brain to spontaneously sense tension through repetition and habit formation.

Like PMR, tension-relaxation has been very useful in treating a variety of illnesses such as hypertension and migraine headaches. As a stress management tool, it's one of the best ways to train yourself to trigger the relaxation response whenever you feel tense or anxious. With practice, you'll be able to start relaxation at any stage of tension you happen to be in without ever having to contract your muscles at all. Depending on your physical and mental abilities, this may take anywhere from two weeks to two months. When you finally reach that stage, you'll have accomplished your goal of making relaxation a natural and spontaneous habit that becomes stronger and stronger every time you relax.

10

Meditation

Meditation has been used for centuries in different parts of the world as a means to achieve deep relaxation and peace of mind. And although some meditative exercises use certain religious words and phrases, meditation in itself is not a religion or a philosophy. Rather, it's a tool that uses our internal awareness and our mind to release tension and bring about relaxation, tranquility, and inner peace. Relaxation, therefore, is not the same as meditation but is the consequence or end result of meditative techniques.

According to Dr. Herbert Benson, professor of medicine at Harvard Medical School and author of *The Relaxation Response,* there are four basic elements that are necessary for achieving deep relaxation through meditation. These are:

1. A quiet, peaceful environment. Just like any other stress management exercise that produces relaxation, meditation requires solitude and comfort. Distractions must be avoided completely, perhaps more so than with any other technique because concentration is the most basic component of meditation.

   When choosing a place to meditate, make sure you find someplace that will be free from distractions for the entire length of your exercise. It may be a quiet room, a peaceful backyard, a church, or even the woods. The important thing is to make sure that you won't be distracted in the middle of your meditation.

2. A decreased muscle tone. Comfort is critical since any undue muscle tenseness will interfere with concentration. The best positions for meditation are the cross-legged sitting position on a firm pillow, mattress, or rug, or a normal sitting position on a

straight, comfortable chair with your head, neck, and back straight. Other positions, such as fully or semireclined, are not as effective with this particular technique because there's a tendency to become drowsy and fall asleep. And unless your intent is to cure insomnia, you won't get as much out of the exercise as you should. When assuming a sitting position, make sure you don't sit in such a way that you'll get cramps within a few minutes. If you can't sit comfortably with your legs crossed, then just sit any way that makes you feel relaxed and loose.

3. A passive attitude. This is probably the most important of the four elements because successful meditation requires that you not guide or direct your thoughts but let them go freely and passively. Nothing is more distracting during meditation than to think about everything that goes through your mind. When distracting thoughts do pop in, try to disregard them. Don't be too concerned about whether or not they're affecting your meditation exercise. The worst thing you can do at this point is to worry about how you're performing. Remain calm and passive and let distracting thoughts float away by themselves. The way to do this is through a mental device.

4. A mental device. In order to help concentration and keep distracting thoughts from interfering with meditation, you need to use a constant stimulus to focus on. A mental device is an object to dwell upon such as a sound, a word, a syllable, or a phrase which is repeated over and over during the course of the exercise. Because total concentration is one of the more difficult tasks we can encounter, using a mental device or a "mantra" allows us to break distracting thoughts and reach deeper levels of internal awareness.

    When choosing a mental device, don't choose one that will cause you to think about it rather than on the meditation itself. Choose one that will create a feeling of peace, tranquility, and relaxation and make you forget about the mechanics of the technique. Only you can decide what's best for you, either through practice or by trial and error. Whatever mantra you choose, make sure it's the one that frees you from outside forces. Some examples and suggestions are discussed later in the chapter.

Meditative Breathing

The manner in which we breath during relaxation is very important because of the close relationship between our respiratory and central nervous systems. It's well known that breathing rates and breathing patterns have a profound effect on brain waves, which in turn influence both our mental and physical processes. Improper or intermittent breathing, for example, can disrupt biochemical reactions, alter emotional states, and create anxiety. For this reason, an integral part of any meditative exercise is properly controlled breathing. Here are two simple breathing exercises that should help enhance not only meditation but any other relaxation exercise.

Exercise #1—Diaphragm Breathing

This exercise was initially described in the chapter on progressive muscle relaxation, but I'll summarize it again here. While sitting in a meditative position, place your right hand on your diaphragm just above your waist and your left hand on your upper chest. As you breathe deeply, your right hand should be pushed out and in with each inhalation and exhalation while your left hand remains steady. If you're breathing properly, air will travel into your body without disrupting the muscles in your chest cavity. The advantage of diaphragm breathing is that it's much smoother and more rhythmic than chest breathing. This smooth and rhythmic breathing pattern facilitates concentration and induces relaxation because it's more natural and requires less work.

When practicing diaphragm breathing, make certain that your breaths are smooth and even, without pauses, jerks, or altered tempo. The smoother and more even your breathing is, the more effectively the rest of your body will respond and relax. With a little effort and practice, you'll be able to change your "unnatural" habit of chest breathing to a "natural" habit of diaphragm breathing.

Exercise #2—Timed Breathing

There are two ways to practice timed breathing—both of which improve breathe control and enhance relaxation. And whether you use one or both methods, make an effort to practice regularly in order to condition yourself to inhale and exhale without effort.

Uneven Breathing: In contrast to regular, even breathing, which involves inhalation and exhalation of the same length, uneven breathing requires that you exhale for longer periods of time than you inhale. You do this by slowing down the rate of exhalation until it's approximately two to three times as long as the rate of inhalation. For example, without changing the smoothness or rhythm of your breathing pattern, inhale for two seconds and exhale for four, or inhale for two and exhale for six. Make breathing effortless, eliminating even the pauses between inhalation and exhalation.

Deep Breathing: This exercise will help increase your breathe and body control, which in turn will lead to deeper relaxation and tension relief. Take a deep breath (four to six seconds) using your diaphragm and hold it for a full ten seconds. Then, after taking a few regular breaths, take a deep breath, and while holding your breath, pull your diaphragm back into your spine as far as you can for a full ten seconds. Repeat this exercise several times a day, always remembering to breathe smoothly and effortlessly each time you inhale or exhale.

Breathing exercises are important to meditation because they help bring balance between the central nervous and respiratory systems. In order to achieve deep relaxation through meditation, we need to ensure that these two systems are "in sync," with the central nervous system controlling the flow of the breathing pattern. Practicing these breathing exercises conditions us to use our respiratory system more efficiently and more rhythmically.

Meditative Techniques

The following are various meditative techniques that can be used to trigger the relaxation response. Try them all and then choose the one that best fits your personality and lifestyle. If you're not a religious person, you may not want to use a meditative technique that uses a religious word or phrase. On the other hand, if you are a religious person, meditation may be more effective and meaningful if it does involve a religious word or phrase. Whichever technique you choose, make sure it's the one that allows you to concentrate and become relaxed with the least amount of effort and the least number of distractions.

Meditative Exercise #1

Sit quietly in a comfortable position, close your eyes, and breathe through your nose. Become aware of your breathing pattern, and as you breathe out, say the word "relax" or "one" silently to yourself. Continue doing this for twenty minutes or so. When you finish, sit quietly for several minutes, at first with your eyes closed and gradually with your eyes open. Maintain a relaxed state throughout the exercise and allow relaxation to occur at its own pace.

Meditative Exercise #2

An example of a religious meditation is a repetitive prayer used by Christians as early as the fourteenth century. It's called "The Prayer of the Heart." Sit down alone, in a comfortable position, and in total silence. Lower your head, shut your eyes, and begin breathing gently and rhythmically while you imagine yourself looking into your own heart. Visualize your heart, and as you breathe out say "Lord Jesus, have mercy on me," or "God, grant me peace." Keep repeating this phrase over and over again each time you breathe out. If you like, you can change the phrase or use any phrase that suits your own personal attitudes and needs.

Meditative Exercise #3

This meditative exercise makes use of a rhythmic sound that you can focus on to time your breathing rate and to enhance concentration. Adjust a metronome to a slow setting, say 40 to 60 beats per minute and then begin an even breathing pattern that follows the beat of the metronome. Once your breathing pattern is established and you've begun concentrating on the click of the metronome, say the word "relax" at the same pace as both breathing and clicking. After doing this exercise for several weeks, your brain will automatically associate the metronome's beats with relaxation. Soon, you'll condition yourself to relax instantly because the metronome will act as a subconscious stimulus or cue that triggers the relaxation response.

Meditative Exercise #4

This meditative technique is also called autosuggestion because it uses some of the principles of self-induced hypnosis, although to a much lesser extent. Sit comfortably in a chair facing a wall about six to eight feet away. Pick a spot or an object on the wall (or place one there) that's about a foot above eye level. As you stare at the focal point, breathe slowly and rhythmically. Starting with the number ten, begin counting backwards, one number for each exhalation. As you count, continue to concentrate on the focal point and begin to feel your body getting more and more relaxed.

Soon after beginning the exercise, your eyelids will become heavier and start to blink. When that happens, just let them close. While your eyes are closed, continue counting, but now visualize the numbers in your mind as you say them silently. When you finally reach the number one, remain relaxed and let yourself feel free and easy. Remain in that position for ten to twenty minutes. When you're ready to come out, count from one to three. At one, prepare yourself; at two, take a deep breath; at three, open your eyes, stand up, and stretch.

Practicing this exercise will condition your brain to associate certain numbers (which act as cues) with certain stages of relaxation. Depending on your own individual pattern, number six may stimulate eye closing, number four may stimulate upper body relaxation, and number one may stimulate complete relaxation. The object of this meditation is to induce the relaxation response by suggesting to ourselves that certain numbers stimulate certain relaxation states.

Meditation can be a very effective tool in stress management because it teaches us to not only relax but to focus away from stressful thoughts and feelings. As long as we don't overdo it by meditating for hours on end, meditative exercises are safe and pleasurable; they bring balance to our body and peace to our mind. But most of all, they condition us to relax spontaneously by using devises such as sounds and objects as stimuli which trigger the relaxation response. Meditation has been around for centuries, bringing inner peace and tranquility to people of all religions and philosophies. We too can experience that peace and tranquility by using the power of our mind to eliminate the stresses in our body.

11

Imaging Techniques
and Self-Healing

Imaging—also known as visualization or imaginal relaxation—makes use of mental images as a means of achieving a deeply relaxed state. After meditation, it's probably one of the oldest relaxation techniques practiced by mankind. In this type of exercise, vivid images associated with rest, tranquility, and serenity are used as positive feedback messages to the rest of the body. These images act as cues which stimulate the nervous system and cause tense muscles to respond subconsciously. Once practiced, imaging can be one of the simplest and most enjoyable of all relaxation techniques. And like other relaxation techniques, it too acts as a tool for triggering the relaxation response—in this case, by conditioning the brain to associate mental images with relaxation.

Imaging has also been used as a method for inducing self-healing. Because of its ability to shift the body's immune system into high gear, imaging has been used successfully to help treat various types of cancers as well as other diseases linked to a breakdown in the immune response. In combination with radiation or chemotherapy treatments, the use of imaging has resulted in much higher survival rates than with the use of treatments alone. This happens because "Natural Killer" cells, which are special cells that seek out and attack all types of cancer cells, are stimulated when the body is relaxed. Self-healing is possible when we allow the power of our brain to keep our immune system going at full force during those times when we need it most.

There are many different kinds of imaging exercises. The type of imaging you do will depend on your personality and your experiences, as well as your likes and dislikes. But regardless of the imaging exercises you choose, you need to follow certain guidelines that will make them much more successful and enjoyable. These are:

1. Make comfort a priority before starting an exercise. It's almost impossible to maintain a positive image for any length of time unless you're relaxed and comfortable throughout the imaging session. Any tensions that arise will have a tendency to block or at least affect your concentration and, therefore, disrupt your image.

2. Make sure that the mental images you choose always "fit" your own idea of what's truly relaxing to you. If you hate the beach, for example, you shouldn't use an image of sand and sea as a relaxation device no matter how relaxing other people think it is. On the other hand, if you find a cool, lush green forest refreshing and relaxing, then use that as a mental image. Always use an activity, scene, or picture that makes you feel the most relaxed and gives you the greatest sense of pleasure and comfort. You're the only one who can do that.

3. Start each imaging exercise with relaxed and smooth breathing. Imaging is much easier once your mind and body are in the process of becoming relaxed. As you breathe and relax, concentrate on the evenness of your breath first and then begin visualizing. If you have trouble keeping an image in your mind, you need to reevaluate whether or not your chosen image is indeed the right one for you. There may be something in your image that's causing distractions or discomfort. If another image keeps cropping up in your mind, perhaps from your childhood or from a past vacation, then that particular image may be stronger and more effective than the one you've chosen. With practice, you'll be able to establish an image that's exactly right for you. Therefore, don't ignore images that keep popping into your mind if you find that they make you feel relaxed and peaceful.

4. Choose images that are vivid, real, and meaningful. Most of us have an idea of what we think the perfect image should be, but in most cases these fantasy images tend to become blurred and intermittent. The best images come from your own real experiences. Therefore, choose an image that you've experienced and enjoyed; one that has given you pleasure and peace. Because they're part of your stored memory, real images become more vivid and long-lasting and will serve you well time and time again.

Imaging Exercises Used For Relaxation

There are literally thousands of examples of imaging exercises, each one as unique as the individual doing it. I'm going to give several examples here with the idea that you'll take the basic outline, change it if you like, and incorporate your own "personal image" into it. Although you may want to use one of the exercises given here, you should be aware of your own personal needs and desires in order for this stress management tool to work for you. Remember, it's very important for an image to "fit the individual" and not the other way around.

Imaging Exercise #1

Select a comfortable position, close your eyes, and begin breathing slowly and smoothly. With each breath, feel the muscles in your body becoming heavier and heavier. Imagine the tension melting away as you continue breathing rhythmically and naturally. Now picture yourself lying on a warm, tropical beach basking in the glow of an afternoon sun. Visualize the vivid, beautiful colors of the sky, the earth, the flowers, and the plants around you. As you lie on the beach, the warmth of the golden sand penetrates every pore of your body and makes you feel warmer and warmer. The golden sand feels soft and soothing; its warmth enters your hands and feet and begins to creep throughout your entire body. Imagine yourself lying serenely and restfully as your muscles become loose and limp. Feel your body sinking into the sand and drifting deeper and deeper into a state of peace and total relaxation. With each breath, watch your body become more and more relaxed, more and more at peace.

Now feel the warmth of the sunlight all over your body, warming you deeply and gently. Visualize the inside of your body bathed in the golden light, absorbing every ray and glowing as radiantly as the sun. A warm, gentle breeze swirls around your body and warms you even more. Visualize and feel the breeze blowing over every part of your body.

As you visualize these images, it may help to say to yourself: "I feel warm and relaxed, "I feel the warmth spreading throughout my body," or "the warmth of the sand is making my muscles feel so loose and relaxed." Continue the imaging exercise for about 20 minutes or so and then gradually become more alert, saying to yourself 3 times "I feel refreshed and relaxed." Slowly open your eyes, take a few deep breaths, and stretch for a few seconds.

Imaging Exercise #2

Select a comfortable position, close your eyes, and begin a smooth rhythmic breathing pattern. Continue breathing this way for a few minutes and then visualize a picturesque lagoon surrounded by tall palm trees and beautiful flowers. The water is a clear, blue turquoise and overhead is a blue cloudless sky. You hear nothing but the soft whisper of a breeze as it gently passes over your body and touches your face with its light invisible fingers.

Imagine yourself floating on the calm, gentle water. As you float, the warm water soothes and relaxes your muscles. Feel the water massaging first your feet, then your legs, your arms, and finally the rest of your body. The water becomes warmer and warmer, and as you drift deeper and deeper into a relaxed state, it begins to melt the tension away. Picture yourself absolutely weightless in the water, perfectly at peace and floating gently, smoothly, and slowly. You're one with the water; it surrounds you completely and loosens every muscle in your body. Each time you breath, the warm, soothing water lifts you slightly; and each time you sink back down, more tension is melted away. Soon, your body is so relaxed in the water that you feel like you're a part of it.

You can do this exercise in a relaxed sitting or lying position, or while taking a warm bath. A word of caution when doing this in a bathtub, however. Since this technique will make you feel so relaxed, you may have a tendency to doze off. Make sure your head is propped up with a float or something else that will prevent your head from slipping down into the water. A sudden jolt like that can ruin your next attempt at visualizing. Continue the exercise for about twenty minutes and then visualize yourself slowly floating to shore. Gradually get out of the water saying to yourself "I feel so refreshed and relaxed." Open your eyes, stand up slowly, and stretch for a few seconds.

Imaging and Self-Healing

For those of us suffering with illness and disease, the body is often regarded as the enemy. Negative feelings and attitudes are quite common during those trying times because we tend to start thinking of our body as a source of distress rather than a source of health and pleasure. We develop fears and anxieties which become worse and worse and lead to ever spiraling cycles of depression and hopelessness. And we give up on ourselves because we just can't believe that the body which was responsible for the disease in the first place is able to fight it at the same time. Creating positive beliefs through imaging, however, can reverse that cycle of fear and depression. Imaging can actually stimulate our immune system to rise up and fight disease head on!

The benefits of imaginal self-healing result from our positive expectations and attitudes toward illness. Together with traditional medical treatment, which should always be a primary source of therapy, imaging can have a tremendous effect on reversing the disease process while creating a mental environment that enhances the healing process. In summary, self-healing exercises are effective because they:

1. Reduce the fear and depression of knowing that our body has been taken over by illness. By regaining a sense of control over our body's immune functions, we develop a more favorable outlook on our health, renew our energy levels, and establish a better perspective on life.

2. Bring about positive physical changes within our immune, endocrine, cardiovascular, and nervous systems. These changes act together to help fight illness and strengthen our ability to resist disease.

3. Condition our brain to respond to illness and disease in a natural and direct way. The process of relaxation by itself can decrease stress and tension to the point of completely altering bodily functions so they work for us instead of against us. By using the power of our mind to help fight disease, we enhance our ability to regain health and vitality.

The following is an example of an imaging exercise used for general self-healing. Later, I'll discuss more specific imaging exercises that have been used very successfully by cancer specialists for treating patients with various types of cancer.

General Self-Healing Imaging Exercise

Begin this exercise as you would any other imaging exercise—in a comfortable position, with your eyes closed, and with an even, rhythmic breathing pattern. Deepen your relaxation by breathing slowly and counting down from ten to one, one number for every exhalation. As you count, release more tension and allow your body to become heavier and more relaxed. You can also use the progressive muscle relaxation technique or the tension-relaxation technique if you wish in order to get yourself into a deeply relaxed state. Once you feel deeply relaxed, visualize the part of your body that's a source of ill-health or discomfort. Try to be as vivid as possible. Consult a medical text or guide beforehand if you're not sure of what a specific organ or body part looks like. According to some therapists, the more vivid, detailed, and accurate your image is, the better your chances will be of using this technique successfully.

As you relax and breathe slowly, see the organ or body part clearly and vividly in your mind. Watch the blood circulating through that organ, bringing with it oxygen and nutrients that enrich and heal, energize and invigorate. With every breath you take, visualize more and more warm, life-giving blood flowing into the organ or body part and removing toxic wastes and damaged cells. See the organ glow red with health and vitality and picture yourself in perfect health with no sign of disease or illness. Continue this mental imaging for about twenty minutes before slowly opening your eyes and stretching.

You can use this mental imagery more specifically by visualizing the actual organ or body part that's the source of illness. For example, if stomach or intestinal ulcers are the problem, you might visualize them as being covered and repaired by new cells. Warm, healthy blood flows over the damaged areas bringing with it the new, healthy cells which attach and grow over the ulcers. As more and more life-giving blood flows over the damaged areas, they become healthier and more ulcer free. Next, visualize yourself completely free of ulcers, enjoying life as a happy and stress free person.

Almost any illness or disease can be visualized this way with good success as long as you don't expect instant results. You have to remember that mental imaging is a process of visualizing a "desired outcome" and not an instant miracle cure. So, although it's very important to have a positive image and actually see yourself becoming well, it's also important to realize that imaging is an ongoing process that moves you steadily toward the end result. The value of this positive attitude and positive image is so great that anything less won't be as effective and may even cause anxiety and frustration. Therefore, for optimum results, you need to always visualize not only the process of healing but the positive and successful end result as well.

Imaging and Cancer Treatment

In the early 1970s, a unique method of cancer treatment was attempted which involved both standard treatment and visualization exercises. Patients were instructed to relax deeply while mentally picturing the cancer being destroyed by their body's own immune system. In numerous cases, cancers that had very low cure rates when treated with radiation or chemotherapy alone were completely arrested by combining the treatment with relaxation and visualization. It should be emphasized, however, that relaxation and visualization were never meant to be a substitute for traditional therapy but rather an adjunct that enhanced the healing process through increased immunity. And since cancer is basically a breakdown of our body's immune response, anything that boosts that immune response can have a positive effect on destroying cancer cells.

There are three important steps in helping treat cancer through visualization: 1) achieving a deeply relaxed state, 2) visualizing the specific cancer within a specific body part, and 3) visualizing the treatment being used successfully to attack the cancer. It's very important to focus on proper breathing and become deeply relaxed at the start of each self-healing session. The progressive muscle relaxation or tension-relaxation techniques discussed in previous chapters may be used in order to achieve a deeply relaxed state. Or, you can use any method of relaxation you choose so long as your body becomes deeply relaxed and tension free before actually beginning the imaging process. Once relaxation is achieved, you can begin visualizing the specific cancer in any way you choose (as a shapeless form, as a cell with projecting fingers, as a cell with teeth, etc.). You can think of it as a group of weak and helpless cells which are normally destroyed by our body many times during the course of a lifetime. If you remember, each one of us is susceptible to and probably develops some kind of cancer growth. It's during our more susceptible times that we need to help our immune system fight that cancer growth in a new and powerful way.

Next, picture in your mind the treatment that will attack and destroy those weak cancer cells. If radiation treatment is used, imagine laser beams or spurts of energy hitting these cancer cells and destroying them. The dead cells are then attacked by an army of strong and aggressive white blood cells which swallow them up and carry them away from healthy tissue. The normal cells repair the damage and continue to thrive. If the treatment is chemotherapy, imagine the chemical distributing itself among the cancer cells, poisoning them as they come into contact with it. Because the cancer cells are weak and helpless, they're destroyed while the normal healthy cells continue to grow and become healthier.

The best results have been achieved when cancer patients performed these exercises three times a day for at least fifteen minutes at a time. With both radiation and chemotherapy, it's also important to visualize the cancer shrinking and responding in a positive way while at the same time visualizing the normal cells becoming healthier and healthier. Imagine yourself free of pain, free of disease, and full of life, energy, and vigor. Rather than focusing on the negative side of your illness, focus on your body healing itself and becoming well again. This positive visualization will improve attitude, enhance relaxation, mobilize the immune system, and as a result, enhance the healing process.

Creating Powerful Self-Healing Images

When a study was done with cancer patients who practiced imaging, it was discovered that the patients who used weak or negative images were much less successful than those who used strong, positive images. This discovery proved that the image itself is an important factor in the healing process. According to Dr. Simonton of the University of Oregon Medical Center, Department of Radiation Oncology, there are certain imagery features which are most effective when treating cancer. These strong images are effective because they represent a strong belief in recovery, which in itself is critical for proper health and well-being. The features that create these effective and powerful self-healing images are:

1. *A strong and powerful treatment.* Most of us tend to think of cancer as a powerful disease that takes over our body during a time of weakness. Therefore, we must think of the treatment as something that's clearly stronger and powerful enough to destroy any cancer. It's also helpful to think of the treatment as something good and supportive. Some cancer patients have gone so far as to personalize their treatment by giving it a name. Thinking of a treatment such as radiation in this way makes it seem less intimidating and fearful.

   The image can be made even stronger if we make a vivid distinction between it and the cancer. Using a bland, neutral color such as gray or light brown for the cancer and a vivid color such as red or yellow for the treatment makes it easier to visualize the treatment as a dominant force that can destroy cancer cells.

2. *Weak and helpless cancer cells.* Rather than thinking of cancer cells as being able to grow and multiply, it's extremely important to visualize them as weak and powerless. It might help to imagine cancer cells as soft or fragile, not capable of standing up to the treatment. Never give cancer cells the colors black, red, or orange. These colors tend to stimulate strong emotions. Instead, give them a color such as gray in order to give them a weak and impotent appearance.

3. *Normal and healthy, noncancerouse cells.* The very nature of cancer treatment dictates that the treatment will affect both cancerous and noncancerous cells. Therefore, you need to visualize the normal, noncancerous cells being strong and healthy enough to recover from any damage that the treatment might do to them. So, while the weak and helpless cancer cells are being completely destroyed, the strong and healthy noncancerous cells are quickly being repaired and returned to a normal, healthy condition.

4. *Strong and aggressive white blood cells.* The soldiers of our immune system are the white blood cells. They seek out and destroy foreign bodies that break through our lines of defense. Because they play such an important role in fighting cancer, white blood cells should be visualized as strong, powerful, and aggressive. They must overwhelm cancer cells with their vast numbers and destroy them completely. After the white blood cells do their job, the dead cancer cells should be seen being flushed completely out of the body. This act of flushing out dead cancer cells is very important since many of us have a subconscious fear that even dead cancer cells, if left around long enough, can become menacing again.

   The most powerful images are ones in which the cancer cells are significantly outnumbered and overwhelmed by white blood cells. The image of the white blood cells needs to be as vivid, if not more vivid, than the image of the cancer cells in order to establish the belief that the body's defenses are much more potent than the body's diseases. These may be the most important images you can have because it's now believed that the body's basic shield against cancer is it's own immune system.

5. *A healthy, cancer free body.* Since an important part of imaging is visualizing a desired final outcome, it's important to actually see a positive end result. You need to see yourself as healthy, happy, energized, and most importantly cancer free. If you have trouble visualizing this, you probably don't believe you can recover. Try to see yourself doing all the things you would normally do at your healthiest time of life and force yourself to visually engage in happy activities. It's critical to set a goal for yourself in which you expect to regain health and overcome your battle with cancer. Take control of your image, be assertive in your positive thinking, and express total confidence in your body's ability to heal. This positive image of a successful end result forces you to focus on the healing process and reaffirms the confidence you have that your body will eventually win out over illness.

The concept behind imaging is that total muscle relaxation and even self-healing are possible through the use of a simple mental tool—in this case an image. This mental tool gives us the power to trigger the relaxation response, maintain health, and stimulate the natural healing process within us. Again, we should never use imaging as the sole method of healing or disease therapy. Serious illnesses should always be treated by traditional methods, with relaxation and imaging used as important and beneficial aids in the overall treatment process. Each time you practice imaging, it will become easier to do and much more effective. Within a few weeks, you should be able to achieve deep relaxation and begin vivid imaging within a minute or so of starting an exercise.

The benefits of relaxation and imaging have been so great and the success rate so promising that more and more physicians are beginning to use this combined treatment as a means of enhancing therapy for a variety of illnesses and diseases. Practiced regularly in the comfort of your own home, imaginal relaxation is one of the simplest and most effective ways to relieve stress, maintain good health, and keep the immune system in a state of constant alert. As more and more is learned about how we respond to stress and about our body's natural defense system, we begin to discover that our body has an extraordinary power and ability to not only cope with day to day events, but to literally heal itself in the process.

PART III

SELF-HELP STRESS TESTS AND EVALUATIONS

PART III

SELF-HELP STRESS TESTS

AND EVALUATIONS

12

Stress Charts & Tension Targets

On the next six pages are four weekly stress charts followed by diagrams of muscle areas that are sources of tension. Place a dot in every time slot during which a stress symptom occurs. After four weeks, compare the charts and see when stress occurs most often. Those are the times and the days when you should be especially aware of stress reactions. Use these charts along with your stress diary to pinpoint times of stress. In the muscle area diagrams, place a dot within the square that corresponds to aches or pains. Concentrate on those areas when doing relaxation exercises.

Week 1

	Sun	Mon	Tue	Wed	Thur	Fri	Sat
7am							
8am							
9am							
10am							
11am							
12n							
1pm							
2pm							
3pm							
4pm							
5pm							
6pm							
7pm							
8pm							

Week 2

	Sun	Mon	Tue	Wed	Thur	Fri	Sat
7am							
8am							
9am							
10am							
11am							
12n							
1pm							
2pm							
3pm							
4pm							
5pm							
6pm							
7pm							
8pm							

Week 3

	Sun	Mon	Tue	Wed	Thur	Fri	Sat
7am							
8am							
9am							
10am							
11am							
12n							
1pm							
2pm							
3pm							
4pm							
5pm							
6pm							
7pm							
8pm							

Week 4

	Sun	Mon	Tue	Wed	Thur	Fri	Sat
7am							
8am							
9am							
10am							
11am							
12n							
1pm							
2pm							
3pm							
4pm							
5pm							
6pm							
7pm							
8pm							

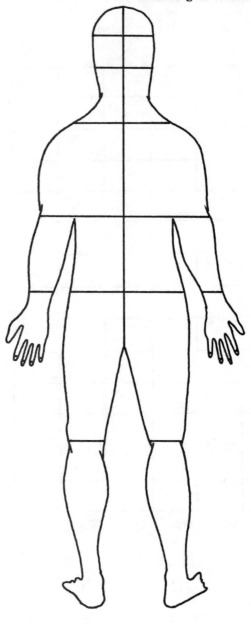

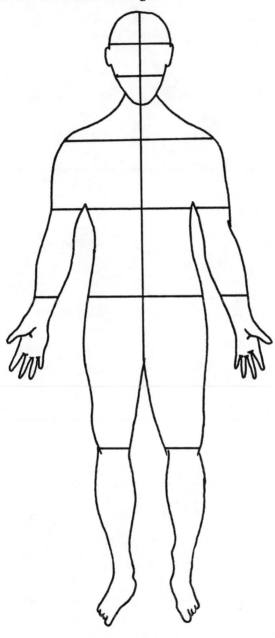

13

Testing Your Stress Knowledge

How much more do you know about stress and how it affects you? The following stress tests are meant to reinforce your knowledge of stress and coping strategies and make you more aware of stress management as a tool for better living. If you answer a question incorrectly, go back to the section of the book that deals with that aspect of stress and read it once again. It's important to review those areas that you're unsure of in order to make stress management a complete and effective method for relieving the stress and anxiety in your life. If you answer all or most of the questions correctly, you can take heart in the fact that you're now your own stress expert and well on your way to becoming healthier and more stress free.

Facts About Stress

	TRUE	FALSE
1. People react to emotional stress just as easily as they do to physical stress.	____	____
2. Constant arousal due to stress can cause a person's blood pressure to remain low.	____	____
3. Stress due to overload can result from demands that occur at home.	____	____
4. An individual who is adjusting to many life changes in a short period of time is less likely than usual to become ill.	____	____

5. Thinking about an unpleasant event is never as stressful as actually experiencing that event.   ____ ____

6. Thinking of oneself as useless and powerless can increase one's stress level.   ____ ____

7. The most stressful situations are usually those over which people feel they have a great deal of control.   ____ ____

8. Stress may decrease the body's ability to defend itself against disease.   ____ ____

9. Severe stress may cause people to have accidents.   ____ ____

10. People who have Type A personalities are more likely to suffer from stress reactions.   ____ ____

11. One of the most common traits of Type A personality is doing only one thing at a time.   ____ ____

12. Excessive stress affects the body's ability to utilize nutrients such as vitamins and minerals.   ____ ____

13. A person under stress may feel confused.   ____ ____

14. Overload occurs when people are able to meet the demands which are placed on them.   ____ ____

15. A person under stress is usually able to perform tasks better than usual.   ____ ____

16. Some degree of stress is necessary for life.   ____ ____

17. Stress disorders are caused by constant stress arousal, leading to organ system failure. ___ ___

18. Too much stimulation is always more stressful than too little. ___ ___

19. The stress produced by a situation depends more on the situation than on the person's perception of the situation. ___ ___

20. The Type A personality is associated with heart disease. ___ ___

21. The best level of stress is that amount which improves a person's performance without producing harmful side effects. ___ ___

22. Frustration occurs when individuals lack the ability to take necessary actions or when their actions are blocked by external obstacles. ___ ___

23. Favorable life changes are never as stressful as unfavorable life changes. ___ ___

24. The amount of stress individuals feel when in a crowd depends on how much control they think they have in the situation and on their cultural background. ___ ___

25. An individuals reaction to stressors is determined by that person's prior attitudes, experiences, values, and even religion. ___ ___

26. Thinking of oneself as helpless and worthless can lead to increased stress. ___ ___

27. An individual's expectation about a stressful event can influence the individual's stress level significantly. ___ ___

28. Physiological responses to stressors   ____   ____
    occur automatically, without very much
    conscious thought.

29. Hormones released under stress remain   ____   ____
    in the body for only a short period of
    time.

30. Arthritis and cancer may be indirectly   ____   ____
    related to stress.

31. A person under stress doesn't usually   ____   ____
    return to old habits if they're in-
    appropriate to the present situation.

32. An individual's stress level can increase   ____   ____
    if that individual receives no informa-
    tion or false information about a poten-
    tially stressful event prior to its
    occurrence.

33. During prolonged stress, the body en-   ____   ____
    ters a phase in which everything re-
    turns to a normal level of functioning
    without any symptom of stress.

34. Mental health problems, such as   ____   ____
    depression, should never be treated as
    emotional stress responses.

35. There is no evidence that stress causes   ____   ____
    an acceleration of the aging process.

36. Many cases of sexual dysfunction, such   ____   ____
    as impotence, frigidity, and premature
    ejaculation are a direct result of stress.

37. The body can be conditioned to relax   ____   ____
    just as quickly and easily as it's con-
    ditioned to tense up during stress.

38. One of the biggest sources of stress is   ____   ____
    the inability to make use of time.

39. Diet and nutrition are not very impor-   ____   ____
    tant factors in stress reactions.

40. Muscles that are constantly contracted   ____   ____
    lead to increased anxiety and emotional
    stress.

Scoring Key:
(1) T   (2) F   (3) T   (4) F   (5) F   (6) T   (7) F
(8) T   (9) T   (10) T   (11) F   (12) T   (13) T   (14) F
(15) F   (16) T   (17) T   (18) F   (19) F   (20) T   (21) T
(22) T   (23) F   (24) T   (25) T   (26) T   (27) T   (28) T
(29) F   (30) T   (31) F   (32) T   (33) T (34) F   (35) F
(36) T   (37) T   (38) T   (39) F   (40) T

Total Number Correct _____   35—40 = Excellent
                                        30—34 = Good
                                        25—29 = Fair
                                        Less than 25 = Poor

Coping With Stress

	TRUE	FALSE
1. Imagining heaviness and warmth in one's body parts is an effective relaxation technique.	____	____
2. An individual should consume more caffeine during stressful times.	____	____
3. Competitive physical activity is an effective stress management strategy.	____	____
4. Involvement in the pleasure of physical activity leads to feelings of well-being.	____	____
5. Breaking down complicated tasks into smaller parts can reduce stress.	____	____
6. Stress can be reduced by avoiding routines whenever possible.	____	____

7. When undergoing important life   ____   ____
    changes, stress can be reduced by in-
    creasing the number of other changes
    that are made.

8. Heartbeat can be monitored through   ____   ____
    biofeedback.

9. Individuals should not try to change   ____   ____
    their relation to stressors.

10. Sitting comfortably helps to quiet one's ____   ____
    internal environment.

11. Progressive muscle relaxation is an   ____   ____
    effective technique for relieving such
    illnesses as hypertension and ulcers.

12. Anticipating periods of boredom and   ____   ____
    planning activities for those periods can
    reduce stress.

13. When using physical exercise as a stress ____   ____
    management technique, one should try
    to exert oneself as much as possible.

14. In muscle relaxation exercises, an indi- ____   ____
    vidual attempts to eliminate the
    physical sensations that are associated
    with relaxation.

15. Becoming less competitive with oneself   ____   ____
    and others is an effective way to reduce
    Type A behavior.

16. Delegating authority and responsibility ____   ____
    to others will have no effect on stress.

17. To be effective, relaxation must be used ____   ____
    at the same time and place each time
    it's done.

18. Being in a place away from other people helps to quiet one's internal environment.   ____   ____

19. Focusing on one's positive characteristics improves a person's self-image and reduces stress.   ____   ____

20. Increased muscle activity is a characteristic of relaxation.   ____   ____

21. Individuals shouldn't try to identify the environmental situations that prompt their stress.   ____   __

22. Even if individuals can't change the nature of stressors, they can change their relation to stressors.   ____   ____

23. An effective way to reduce stress is to find alternatives for goals and behaviors that one has been unable to accomplish.   ____   ____

24. Listing tasks in order of their importance so that the most important tasks can be completed first helps to reduce stress.   ____   ____

25. Accepting the fact that no one can do everything perfectly helps to reduce stress.   ____   ____

26. Vacations, even when they involve changes in location, routine, or level of stimulation, are always a good way to relieve stress.   ____   ____

27. Effective relaxation can only be achieved when used regularly and in long spurts.   ____   ____

28. Physical activity that is vigorous
    enough to bring relaxation afterwards
    makes a person less open to the nega-
    tive effects of stress.   ____   ____

29. People should learn exactly what types   ____   ____
    of situations cause them to feel stress.

30. During relaxation, it's impossible to   ____   ____
    feel nervous or anxious.

31. Relaxation happens when a person lets   ____   ____
    it happen instead of forcing it to
    happen.

32. Stress cannot be reduced by anticipat-   ____   ____
    ing periods of boredom and planning
    something stimulating to do during
    those periods.

33. Stress cannot be reduced by estab-   ____   ____
    lishing routines which become
    automatic.

34. Intentionally changing the stressful   ____   ____
    aspects of one's personality can help one
    cope with many kinds of stressors.

35. Developing close friendships with peo-   ____   ____
    ple one can trust reduces stress.

36. One of the best ways to reduce emo-   ____   ____
    tional stress is through social support
    networks.

37. Older people can reduce stress by own-   ____   ____
    ing a pet.

38. Relaxation training allows people to   ____   ____
    regulate bodily processes that they
    thought were beyond conscious control.

39. People who have difficult things to do   ____   ____
increase their stress by setting time
aside for breaks.

40. Sometimes the best way for individuals   ____   ____
to decrease their stress is to avoid
places or situations where they feel
stress.

Scoring Key:
(1) T (2) F (3) F (4) T (5) T (6) F (7) F
(8) T (9) F (10) T (11) T (12) T (13) F (14) F
(15) T (16) F (17) F (18) T (19) T (20) F (21) F
(22) T (23) T (24) T (25) T (26) F (27) F (28) T
(29) T (30) T (31) T (32) F (33) F (34) T (35) T
(36) T (37) T (38) T (39) F (40) T

Total Number Correct _____   35—40 = Excellent
                                 30—34 = Good
                                 25—29 = Fair
                 Less than 25 = Poor

Responses To Stress

1. Valerie has just been promoted to a new job in a different city.
An appropriate way for Valerie to reduce her stress would be:

    A. Change her hairstyle and way of dressing to reflect her
new image.
    B. Take on as much work as she can to keep herself busy.
    C. Establish a suitable schedule soon after she arrives.
    D. Avoid responsibility as much as possible at first.

2. John is in a noisy office and is trying to concentrate on his
work. An appropriate way for John to reduce his stress would
be to:

    A. Skip lunch and work during lunch hour when the office is
quieter.
    B. Rearrange the books and papers on his desk.
    C. Wear more comfortable clothes to work.
    D. Take periodic breaks away from the office to get some
relief.

3. David is worried that he will fail his history test, even though he has studied hard for it. An appropriate way for David to reduce his stress would be to:

   A. Stay up late the night before the test in order to study more.
   B. Think about how angry his parents will be if he fails the test.
   C. Go out and take a bicycle ride.
   D. Get up early the next morning and study some more.

4. Arthur is very busy typing when a co-worker asks him to help her with her typing. An appropriate way for Arthur to reduce his stress would be to:

   A. Help her with her typing but explain that he won't do it again.
   B. Explain that he can't do her typing and concentrate on finishing his own work.
   C. Pretend that his co-worker's request doesn't bother him and continue working.
   D. Tell his co-worker that he'll do her typing after he's finished with his.

5. David has been told that there is no chance that he can pitch for his baseball team because the manager's brother will be taking his place. An appropriate way for Paul to reduce his stress would be to:

   A. Look into pitching for another team.
   B. Get to know the other members of the team better.
   C. Tell the owner that he insists on being able to pitch for the team, no matter what.
   D. Quit pitching altogether.

6. Kathy drives home on a busy, crowded freeway. An appropriate way for Kathy to reduce her stress would be to:

   A. Drive with the car windows open slightly.
   B. Make sure that she takes the same route home whenever possible.
   C. Drink a cup of coffee as she drives.
   D. Try an alternate route or a different time when it's not as crowded.

7. Gary is concerned that the quality of his work is not good enough, even though all of the people he works with tell him he's doing a good job. An appropriate way for Gary to reduce his stress would be to:

   A. Spend more time working to improve the quality of his work.
   B. Plan to have a few beers with his co-workers every day after work.
   C. Spend more time focusing on the positive qualities of his work.
   D. Look for another line of work that would make him more satisfied.

8. Leslie has just recently married and moved to a new city. An appropriate way for Leslie to reduce her stress would be to:

   A. Try to change her old habits.
   B. Set aside some time each day to relax.
   C. Take a vacation with her husband.
   D. Take on extra work to keep her mind busy.

9. Sharon works on an assembly line where she watches metal fittings go by all day long. An appropriate way for Sharon to reduce her stress would be to:

   A. Bring in a soft cushion for her chair.
   B. Ask her boss if she can listen to a radio as she works.
   C. See if she can work through lunch so that she can finish her work as quickly as possible.
   D. Increase her work load to keep her mind occupied.

10. Karen had been planning on taking a week off from work. Now her boss tells Karen that it's impossible for her to have the vacation time she had planned. An appropriate way for Karen to reduce her stress would be to:

   A. Threaten to switch jobs unless she can take her vacation as planned.
   B. Act as if she didn't want the time off that much anyway.
   C. Tell her boss that she's disappointed and ask if she can take the time off next month.

     D.   Act angry enough to convince her boss to give her the time off she wanted.

11. Jennifer has four final exams and only two days left to study for them. An appropriate way for Jennifer to reduce her stress would be to:

     A.   Take her mind off her own tests by helping a friend study.
     B.   Pick the hardest course and study for that exam only.
     C.   Study for each of her tests, one at a time.
     D.   Try to spend twice as much time as she usually does studying for the exams.

12. Gwen wants to be president of a local club but has been told that she lacks the organization ability. An appropriate way for Gwen to reduce her stress would be to:

     A.   Stop attending club meetings.
     B.   Take a business class to improve her skills.
     C.   Tell the club members that she doesn't really want to be the president.
     D.   Accept the fact that she can never be the president.

13. Gregg lives across from an all night gas station and is disturbed by the noise from the cars. An appropriate way for Gregg to reduce his stress would be to:

     A.   Play loud music to block out the noise.
     B.   Take a sleeping pill to help get to sleep.
     C.   Give all of his business to another gas station.
     D.   Use relaxation techniques to help block out noise.

14. Stanley is surrounded by people at a very crowded party. An appropriate way for Stanley to reduce his stress would be to:

     A.   Stay in the middle of the crowd.
     B.   Have several extra glasses of wine in order to relax.
     C.   Loosen his tie so that he will feel more comfortable.
     D.   Get away from the crowd and stay in an area that's more comfortable for him.

15. Joyce must speak to a large group of people and keeps thinking about the time she was giving a speech in front of her class and

forgot what she was to say. An appropriate way for Joyce to reduce her stress would be to:

A. Set aside some time before the speech to relax.
B. Remember as many details as she can about her previous experience giving a speech.
C. Keep her hands busy while she gives the speech.
D. Review her speech until the last minute in order to be better prepared.

Scoring Key:

The responses to the preceding questions fall into one of five response categories. They are:

Appropriate —a response that is correct or appropriate for the situation.
Unhealthy —a response that is unhealthy.
Violation —a response that is in direct violation of the appropriate responses to stress.
Denial —a response that denies the stress or the problem producing the stress.
Ineffective —a response that is related to the situation but is ineffective in reducing stress. It is neither unhealthy, nor in direct violation, nor a denial.

No.	Appropriate	Unhealthy	Violation	Denial	Ineffective
1.	C	—	A	D	B
2.	D	A	—	—	B,C
3.	C	A	B,D	—	—
4.	B	—	A	C	D
5.	A	—	C	—	B,D
6.	D	C	—	—	A,B
7.	C	B	—	—	A,D
8.	B	—	A,C	—	D
9.	B	C	D	—	A
10.	C	—	A,D	B	—
11.	C	—	A,D	—	B
12.	B	—	—	C	A,D
13.	D	B	A	—	C
14.	D	B	A	—	C
15.	A	—	B,D	—	C

Communicating About Stress

1. Michael wants to communicate to his friend that he gets nervous while driving through heavy traffic. The best way for Michael to say this is:

    A. "I get really anxious when I have to drive in heavy traffic."
    B. "Everyone who drives in heavy traffic gets nervous."
    C. "I can't possibly drive home through this traffic without getting nervous."
    D. "You've got to be crazy to drive through this kind of traffic."

2. Martin wants to tell his son that he feels depressed about retiring from the company where he has worked for twenty years. The best way for Martin to say this is:

    A. "You know how I feel about not working anymore."
    B. "I'll be retiring from the company soon."
    C. "I feel sad when I realize I won't be going into work anymore."
    D. "After I retire, I don't think I'll ever be able to work again."

3. Reggie wants to ask his wife to serve herbal tea instead of coffee at night to help him relax. The best way for Reggie to say this is:

    A. "People can't relax if they're served coffee at night."
    B. "You're not being very sensitive to my needs if you continue to serve coffee at night."
    C. "I think it would help me relax if you would serve herb tea after dinner."
    D. "I think I'll have herbal tea at night instead of coffee."

4. Kathy wants to tell her husband she felt nervous during an important interview but happy about being able to keep her cool. The best way for Kathy to say this is:

    A. "Now I'll never have to worry again about getting nervous when I'm in a tight spot."

B. "You know what it means to me to have remained calm during the interview."

C. "I had a good job interview today."

D. "I really feel good about staying calm during my interview today."

5. David wants to tell his friend that he gets anxious when he has to wait in long lines at the bank or in the grocery store. The best way for David to say this is:

A. "You know how annoyed I get when I'm stuck in a long line."

B. "I'm sure everybody hates waiting in long lines."

C. "You must not have much to do if waiting in long lines doesn't bother you."

D. "I get really anxious when I have to wait in a long line."

6. Jennifer has started to meditate every eveni g to help her manage her stress more effectively. She wa i:s to ask her roommate not to interrupt her when she's m: ditating. The best way for Jennifer to say this is:

A. "It's not very considerate of you to interrupt me when I'm meditating."

B. "Please help me out by leaving me alone sometimes."

C. "Please help me manage my stress by not interrupting me while I meditate."

D. "You know how I feel whenever I'm interrupted during meditation."

7. Paul wants to tell David, his co-worker, that he feels good about being able to stay calm during a very busy time at the office. The best way for Paul to say this is:

A. "I feel good about work now."

B. "I was able to keep my cool during that busy time here and I feel good about it."

C. "You know how good it feels to keep your cool during difficult times here in the office."

D. "I'm never going to get anxious during busy days again."

8. Gerald plans to jog in the morning before work as part of his stress managment program. He wants to ask his wife to help him by making sure he doesn't oversleep in the morning. The best way for Gerald to say this is:

   A. "Everyone needs help sticking to a stress management program, so please help me with mine."
   B. "Please help me with my stress management program by making sure I get up on time to go jogging."
   C. "If you really care about my health, you'll help me get up on time to go jogging in the morning."
   D. "Please make sure I don't oversleep in the morning."

9. Jane gets nervous driving to work in traffi. She decides to reduce her stress by riding her bicycle to work instead of taking the car. She wants to tell her friend that she feels good about her decision. The best way for Jane to say this is:

   A. "Everyone should ride their bicycle to work."
   B. "I feel great about riding my bike instead of driving to work."
   C. "You can imagine how good I feel riding my bike to work."
   D. "Riding a bike to work is great."

10. Valerie wants to tell her family that she's nervous about moving away to a different city. The best way for Valerie to say this is:

   A. "There's no way I'll ever feel good about moving."
   B. "You couldn't possibly understand how I feel about moving."
   C. "I feel anxious about moving to another city."
   D. "Moving to a different city can be nerve-racking."

11. Gregg drinks a great deal of coffee at work and notices that it makes him feel nervous. He wants to ask his co-worker to help him drink less coffee by keeping track of the amount of coffee he drinks. The best way for Gregg to say this is:

   A. "Please help me drink less coffee because you know how nervous I get when I drink too much coffee."

B. "Either you're going to keep track of how much coffee I drink or I'm going to be a nervous wreck."

C. "Please help me drink less coffee."

D. "Please keep track of how many cups of coffee I drink because all the coffee I'm drinking is making me nervous

12. Gwen is trying to reduce the stress in her life by setting up a weekly time schedule. She wants to tell her friend Henry that she's very happy about how much calmer she feels since she has started using the schedule. The best way for Gwen to say this is:

A. "You can see how much my time schedule has helped me."

B. "I feel very calm since I started setting up weekly time schedules."

C. "I think everyone should use a weekly time schedule."

D. "I've been much calmer lately."

13. Sheila is trying to consume less sugar as part of her stress management program. She wants to ask her roommate not to offer her anything sweet to eat. The best way for Sheila to say this is:

A. "Please don't offer me anything sweet because I'm trying to eat less sugar."

B. "You don't help me when you offer me sweet foods to eat."

C. "Everyone finds cutting back on sugar difficult, so please help me try to do it."

D. "Please don't give me anything sweet to eat."

14. Victor wants to tell his wife that he feels very nervous every time he thinks about the examination he must take in a few weeks. The best way for Victor to say this is:

A. "This test that I have to take is a pain."

B. "I guess I'll always get nervous about examinations."

C. "You can imagine how nervous I am about the examination."

D. "I get nervous every time I think about taking that examination."

15. Donald wants to tell his family how good he feels since he's started practicing progressive relaxation every day. The best way for Donald to say this is:

A. "You can tell how good I feel since I've started using progressive relaxation."
B. "I feel great about practicing progressive relaxation every day."
C. "You must be blind not to see how good I feel since I've started practicing relaxation."
D. "I've been feeling pretty relaxed lately."

Scoring key:
The manner in which we send verbal messages can have a great deal to do with how we handle stress. A simple one-line statement can either leave us feeling satisfied or make us more anxious. Therefore, it's important to communicate about stress situations in a way that will be both clear and direct. The responses to the preceding questions fall into one of five categories. They are:

Appropriate —a statement that is correct or appropriate for the situation.
Generalized —a statement that is exaggerated or unrealistic.
Assumption —a statement in which the assumption is made that the person you're talking to knows your feelings or the content of your message.
Judgment —a statement that blames or criticizes.
Incomplete —a statement that doesn't provide all the information needed to send a complete message.

No.	Appropriate	Generalized	Assumption	Judgment	Incomplete
1.	A	B,C	—	D	—
2.	C	—	A	—	B,D
3.	C	A	B	—	D
4.	D	A	B	—	C
5.	D	B	A	C	—
6.	C	—	D	A	B
7.	B	D	C	—	A
8.	B	A	—	C	D
9.	B	A	C	—	D
10.	C	A	—	B	D

11.	D	B	A	—	C
12.	B	C	A	—	D
13.	A	C	—	B	D
14.	D	B	C	—	A
15.	B	—	A	C	D

Stress Source and Resistance Survey

The following survey describes various conditions or times when people might feel stress. Read each statement and circle YES or NO to show if you would feel stress at that time. Each time you circle YES, place a number from 0 to 10 to show how certain you are that you could manage the stress from that situation. The 0 to 10 scale corresponds to the following certainty limits.

0	1	2	3	4	5	6	7	8	9	10
Very Uncertain					Somewhat Certain				Very Certain	

Situation	Might you feel stress?	If Yes, how certain are you that you could manage the stress?
1. You're trying to concentrate but you're constantly being interrupted.	YES/NO	_____
2. You have to do a very boring task.	YES/NO	_____
3. You've been thinking about someone who hurt you in the past.	YES/NO	_____
4. You have a neighbor who plays loud music all the time.	YES/NO	_____
5. You have several things to finish in a very short time.	YES/NO	_____

6. You're home by yourself and   YES/NO   _____
   feel lonely.

7. You're in a crowded bus and   YES/NO   _____
   can't get to the exit in time
   for your stop.

8. You keep thinking about an   YES/NO   _____
   unpleasant experience.

9. You've taken on more than   YES/NO   _____
   you can do.

10. You're waiting on the street   YES/NO   _____
    for someone to pick you up,
    and you're getting cold.

11. Although you have plenty of   YES/NO   _____
    time, you're worried you'll be
    late for an important appointment.

12. Your closest friend has left   YES/NO   _____
    town and you feel alone.

13. You're in a room that's   YES/NO   _____
    extremely hot.

14. You must buy a gift for someone   YES/NO   _____
    and the stores are closing.

15. You saw someone being robbed   YES/NO   _____
    and keep imagining that it
    could happen to you.

16. You have to wait for a delivery   YES/NO   _____
    and you have nothing to do.

17. Your friends keep asking you to   YES/NO   _____
    do things you don't want to do.

18. You must get a prescription   YES/NO   _____
    filled and you can't find a
    drug store that's open.

19. You spend a good deal of time in a place that's very noisy. YES/NO _____

20. No matter how hard you've tried, you haven't been able to finish all your work. YES/NO _____

Scoring

1. Add all the numerical certainty scores _____

2. Count all the "YES" responses _____

3. Count all the "NO" responses _____

4. Divide No. 2 by No. 1 _____

5. Add No. 3 to No. 4. for a final score of _____

17–20 = Excellent stress resistance and management ability.

13–16 = Good stress resistance and good management ability.

10–12 = Fair stress resistance and management ability.

0–9 = Poor stress resistance and management ability.

This survey can also be used to indicate the number and types of stress situations in which you feel pressure. Count the number of "YES" responses. The maximum score of 20 indicates that you feel stress in all specified situations. The minimum score of 0 indicates that you feel stress in none of the specified situations.

In addition to an overall score, your responses can also be linked to specific stress sources. To determine the kinds of stresses you're susceptible to, compare the situations to which you responded YES and scored poorly on to the sources of stress below.

Source of Stress	Situations			
Physical stress	4,	10,	13,	19
Frustration	1,	7,	14,	18

Emotional Stress	3,	8,	11,	15
Poor time management	5,	9,	17,	20
Deprivation	2,	6,	12,	16

Stress Management Survey

This survey describes things that people might do to manage stress. Read each statement and circle
YES or NO to show if you intend to do what's described in the item. Each time you circle YES, place a number from 0 to 10 to show how strong your intention is. The 0 to 10 scale corresponds to the following intention limits.

1	2	3	4	5	6	7	8	9	10
Very Weak									Very Strong

	Do you intend to do this?	If YES, how strong is your intention?
1. Find alternatives for goals you've been unable to reach.	YES/NO	_____
2. Stay away from crowded places if they make you feel nervous.	YES/NO	_____
3. Do the most important things first when you have too many things to do.	YES/NO	_____
4. Find interesting things to do when you're bored.	YES/NO	_____
5. Use earplugs when you're in noisy places.	YES/NO	_____
6. Avoid unnecessary changes when you have many other things to do.	YES/NO	_____

7. Look at the positive things in   YES/NO   _____
   yourself and your life.

8. Take one thing at a time.   YES/NO   _____

9. Get plenty of sleep every night.   YES/NO   _____

10. Talk about your problems with   YES/NO   _____
    friends and family.

11. Talk about your problems with   YES/NO   _____
    the people who are involved
    with them.

12. Balance work with relaxing   YES/NO   _____
    activities.

13. Use relaxation techniques.   YES/NO   _____

14. Get regular exercise.   YES/NO   _____

15. Avoid large amounts of caffeine.   YES/NO   _____

16. Try to identify what's causing   YES/NO   _____
    you stress.

17. Accept realistic goal   YES/NO   _____
    for yourself and others.

18. Avoid having many big changes   YES/NO   _____
    come at the same time.

19. Get professional help if you   YES/NO   _____
    feel too much stress.

20. Accept what you cannnot change.   YES/NO   _____

Scoring

This survey can be scored in two ways as follows:

A. Count the number of "YES" responses, disregarding the
   numerical intention scores. The maximum score of 20 means

that you have a strong intention to use a variety of stress management techniques. A score of less than 15 indicates that you may or may not intend to utilize stress management in certain situations. You should evaluate the "NO" responses and determine why you can't.

B. Add all the numerical intention scores that correspond to the "YES" responses and divide the total number by 20 (the total number of items in the survey). The maximum score of 10 indicates a very strong intention to use stress management techniques. A score of 6 or less indicates that you have some work to do on specific areas of stress management and need to reevaluate how important it is for you to manage the stress in your life.

Appendices

APPENDIX A

The Caffeine Scorecard

Caffeine is one of the culprits that can trigger or aggravate stress reactions because it can cause nervousness, insomnia, restlessness, irritability, headaches, irregular heartbeats, and heart palpitations. These "physical signals" throw our body out of balance and can make us feel ill by initiating, irritating, or intensifying stress responses. People who are especially sensitive to caffeine need to watch out for products that will cause caffeine-induced reactions.

The following tables represent the latest caffeine content of various foods, beverages, and drugs. How much caffeine a person consumes depends on one's personal tastes and how certain products, such as coffee or tea are prepared. Thus, averages are given both for various beverages and for ranges of caffeine levels. All caffeine content levels are expressed in milligrams. Source: U.S. Department of Health and Human Services, Food and Drug Administration.

Caffeine Content of Beverages and Foods

Item	Milligrams Caffeine	
	Average	Range
Coffee (5-oz. cup)		
Brewed, drip method	115	60–180
Brewed, percolator	80	40–170
Instant	65	30–120
Decaffeinated, brewed	3	2– 5
Decaffeinated, instant	2	1– 5
Tea (5-oz. cup)		
Brewed, major U.S. brands	40	20– 90
Brewed, imported brands	60	25–110
Instant	30	25– 50
Iced (12-oz. glass)	70	67– 76

Cocoa beverage (5-oz cup)	4	2– 20
Chocolate milk beverage (8 oz.)	5	2– 7
Milk chocolate (1 oz.)	6	1– 15
Dark chocolate, semi-sweet (1 oz.)	20	5– 35
Baker's chocolate (1 oz.)	26	26
Chocolate-flavored syrup (1oz.)	4	4

Caffeine Content of Soft Drinks

Brand	Milligrams Caffeine (12-oz. serving)
Sugar-Free Mr. PIBB	58.8
Mountain Dew	54.0
Mello Yello	52.8
TAB	46.8
Coca-Cola	45.6
Diet Coke	45.6
Shasta Cola	44.4
Shasta Cherry Cola	44.4
Shasta Diet Cola	44.4
Mr. PIBB	40.8
Dr. Pepper	39.6
Sugar-Free Dr. Pepper	39.6
Big Red	38.4
Sugar-Free Big Red	38.4
Pepsi-Cola	38.4
Aspen	36.0
Diet Pepsi	36.0
Pepsi Light	36.0
RC Cola	36.0
Diet Rite	36.0
Kick	31.2
Canada Dry Jamaica Cola	30.0
Canada Dry Diet Cola	1.2

Caffeine Content of Drugs

Caffeine is an ingredient in numerous prescription drugs as well as in more than 1,000 nonprescription drugs. Most often, it's used in weight-control remedies, alertness or stay-awake tablets, headache and pain relief remedies, cold products, and diuretics. When caffeine is an ingredient in one of these products, it's listed on the product label. Some common examples of caffeine-containing drugs are:

Prescription Drugs	Milligrams Caffeine
Cafergot (for migraine headache)	100
Florinal (for tension headache)	40
Soma Compound (pain relief, muscle relaxant)	32
Darvon Compound (pain relief)	32

Nonprescription Drugs

Weight-Control Aids	
Codexin	200
Dex-A-Diet II	200
Dexatrim, Dexatrim Extra Strength	200
Dietac capsules	200
Maximum Strength Appedrine	100
Prolamine	140
Alertness Tablets	
Nodoz	100
Vivarin	200
Analgesic/Pain Relief	
Anacin, Maximum Strength Anacin	32
Excedrin	65
Midol	32
Vanquish	33
Diuretics	
Aqua-Ban	100
Maximum Strength Aqua-Ban Plus	200
Permathene H2 Off	200
Cold/Allergy Remedies	
Coryban-D capsules	30
Triaminicin tablets	30
Dristan Decongestant tablets	16
Dristan A-F Decongestant tablets	16
Duradyne-Forte	30

APPENDIX B

Social Support and Mutual Help Groups

Social support networks and mutual help groups can be one of the best ways for coping with various negative life experiences. The following is a listing of some of the most common support and mutual help groups. Many of these groups publish newsletters and information pamphlets and have local chapters throughout the United States. Write to them and ask for information about their organization.

ALCOHOLICS ANONYMOUS, 468 Park Avenue South, New York, NY 10163. For men and women who share the common problems of alcoholism.

AMERICAN SCHIZOPHRENIA ASSOCIATION, 219 East 31st Street, New York, NY 10016. For persons seeking cure and prevention of schizophrenia.

ASSOCIATION FOR CHILDREN AND ADULTS WITH LEARNING DISABILITIES, 4156 Library Road, Pittsburg, PA 15234. For children with learning disabilities and their parents to share information, obtain referrals, and advocate for changes in educational methods and opportunities.

BATTERERS ANONYMOUS, 1295 NE Street, San Bernardino, CA 92405. Self-help program for men who are abusive to women. Designed to rehabilitate, to develop better ways to cope with abuse, and to teach skills for handling stress.

CANDLELIGHTERS, 2025 Eye Street, N.W., Washington, D.C. 20006. For parents of young children with cancer: peer support.

THE COMPASSIONATE FRIENDS, P.O. Box 1347, Oak Brook, IL 60521. For bereaved parents: peer support.

DEPRESSIVES ANONYMOUS, P.O. Box 1777, Grand Central Station, New York, NY 10077. Self-help organization patterned after Alcoholics Anonymous that helps people deal with anxiety and depression through meetings and sharing of experiences.

DIVORCE ANONYMOUS, P.O. Box 5313, Chicago, IL 60680. For men and women who are divorced and wish to share experiences and help one another with marriage and divorce problems.

DRUGS ANONYMOUS, P.O. Box 473, Ansonia Station, New York, NY 10023. For persons dependent on drugs including tranquilizers, stimulants, analgesics, sedatives, cocaine, and marijuana. Provides emotional support and teaches methods of coping through the Alcoholics Anonymous approach.

EMOTIONS ANONYMOUS, P.O. Box 4245, St. Paul, MN 55104. For persons with emotional problems: a Twelve-Step Program, adapted from the Alcoholics Anonymous Program.

EPILEPSY FOUNDATION, 4351 Garden City Drive, Landover, MD 20785. For epileptics and their families.

FAMILIES ANONYMOUS, P.O. Box 344, Torrance, CA 90501. For concerned relatives and friends of youth with a wide variety of behavioral problems.

GAMBLERS ANONYMOUS, 2703A West 8th Street, Los Angeles, CA 90005. Helps men and women stop gambling.

GRAY PANTHERS, 3635 Chestnut Street, Philadelphia, PA 19104. An intergenerational movement that fights against age discrimination.

JUVENILE DIABETICS FOUNDATION, 29 East 26th Street, New York, NY 10010. For young diabetics and their families.

MAKE TODAY COUNT, P.O. Box 303, Burlington, IA 52601. For persons with cancer and their families.

MUSCULAR DYSTROPHY ASSOCIATION, 810 Seventh Avenue, New York, NY 10019. For muscular dystrophy patients and their families: peer support and advocates for increased research.

NARCOTICS ANONYMOUS, P.O. Box 622, Sun Valley, CA 91352. For narcotic addicts: peer support for recovered addicts.

NATIONAL ALLIANCE FOR THE MENTALLY ILL, 1200 15th Street, N.W., Washington, D.C. 20005. For families and friends of seriously mentally ill individuals: provides information, emotional support, and advocacy through local and state affiliates.

NATIONAL ASSOCIATION OF MATURE PEOPLE, Box 26792, Oklahoma City, OK 73126. For older citizens: educational programs and materials; recreational activities; group travel programs; guidance and counseling; health, life, and auto insurance; prescription drug services.

NATIONAL ASSOCIATION FOR RETARDED CITIZENS, 2501 Avenue J., Arlington, TX 76011. For mentally retarded children and adults and their families: advocates for research and services.

NATIONAL COUNCIL OF SENIOR CITIZENS, 925 15th Street, Washington, D.C. 20005. For older citizens: organization of 4000 senior citizen club associations which offer education and health programs, recreational programs, reduced drug costs, better housing, and other programs to aid senior citizens.

NATIONAL FEDERATION OF THE BLIND, 1629 K Street, N.W., Washington, D.C. 20006. For blind persons and their families: peer support and advocacy.

NATIONAL PARKINSON FOUNDATION, INC., 1501 N.W. 9th Avenue, Miami, FL 33136. For Parkinson's patients and their families.

NATIONAL SOCIETY FOR CHILDREN AND ADULTS WITH AUTISM, 1234 Massachusetts Avenue, N.W., Washington, D.C. 20005. For autistic children and their families: peer support, advocacy for research and treatment.

NATIONAL SUPPORT CENTER FOR FAMILIES OF THE AGING, Box 245, Swarthmore, PA 19801. For the elderly and their families: provides support, encouragement, and assistance to family members responsible for the welfare of an elderly person.

NEUROTICS ANONYMOUS, P.O. Box 4866, Cleveland Park Station, Washington, D.C. 20008. For the mentally and emotionally ill.

OVEREATERS ANONYMOUS, 2190 West 190th Street, Torrance, CA 90504. For overweight persons: peer support and programs to combat compulsive overeating.

PARENTS ANONYMOUS, 22330 Hawthorne, Torrance, CA 90505. For parents of abused children: peer support, information, crisis prevention.

PARENTS WITHOUT PARTNERS, 7910 Woodmont Avenue, Bethesda, MD 20814. For single parents and their children: peer support.

REACH TO RECOVERY, 777 Third Avenue, New York, NY 10017. For women who have had mastectomies: visitation by peers and peer support through local cancer societies.

RECOVERY INC., 116 South Michigan Avenue, Chicago, IL 60603. For former mental patients: peer support.

THEOS FOUNDATION, The Penn Hills Mall Office Bldg., Rm 306, Pittsburg, PA 15235. For the widowed and their families.

TOUGHLOVE, P.O. Box 1069, Doylestown, PA 18901. A network of over 1200 support groups for parents of problem teenagers: local support groups and regional workshops for parents interested in forming local groups.

UNITED CEREBRAL PALSY, 66 East 34th Street, New York, NY 10016. For those with cerebral palsy.

WIDOWED PERSONS, 1909 K Street, N.W., Washington, D.C. 20049. For widows and widowers: peer support.

APPENDIX C

A Guide To Nutrients

A well-nourished person is always better able to cope with the nutritional demands caused by stress than a person who doesn't maintain a "well-balanced" diet. This is because during prolonged stress, there's an alteration in the body's metabolism of vitamins and minerals and a depletion of amino acids from skeletal muscle. Therefore, individuals who are under chronic or severe stress may need to increase their intake of proteins and other nutrients more so than will nonstressed or moderately stressed individuals.

The stress nutrients receiving the most attention have been vitamins. "Stress vitamins" are widely advertised, and manufacturers claim that taking products such as Stress-Tabs or Fortespan increases the body's resistance to stress. Although these products are as good as any other vitamin supplement, there's no evidence at all that taking any particular brand will make someone more resistant to stress. In fact, the danger of toxicity from taking too much of any vitamin supplement is equally great and, instead of reducing stress, may actually enhance it because of severe physical side effects. A good rule of thumb is to eat properly and, if necessary, use only one standard strength multivitamin tablet daily. Under no circumstances should a person load up on megadoses of vitamins thinking that if some are good, more are better. The following table lists all the vitamins, their functions, their main food sources, and toxic side effects from overdose.

Vitamin A—Retinol

Function: Vitamin A is necessary for new cell growth and healthy tissues and is essential for vision in dim light. Besides night blindness, high sensitivity to light, and other eye disorders, vitamin A deficiency can cause rough, dry skin that becomes more susceptible to infection.

Food Sources: Green and yellow vegetables, yellow fruits, liver, eggs, and milk.

Toxic Side Effects: Headache, nausea, vomiting, fatigue, loss of hair and/or nails, bone pain, skin disorders, and liver problems.

Vitamin B1—Thiamin

Function: Vitamin B1 is required for normal digestion, growth, fertility, lactation, the normal functioning of nerve tissue, and carbohydrate metabolism. Deficiency of Vitamin B1 causes beri-beri, a dysfunctioning of the nervous system. Other deficiency problems include loss of appetite, body swelling, heart problems, nausea, vomiting, and spastic muscle contraction throughout the body.

Food Sources: Pork, soybeans, beans, peas, nuts, and enriched and whole grain breads and cereals.

Toxic Side Effects: None reported.

Vitamin B2—Riboflavin

Function: Riboflavin helps the body obtain energy from carbohydrates and proteins. A deficiency causes lip sores and cracks, as well as dimness of vision.

Food Sources: Leafy vegetables, enriched and whole grain breads and cereals, liver, cheese, lean meats, milk, and eggs.

Toxic Side Effects: None reported.

Niacin

Function: Niacin is necessary for the healthy condition of all tissue cells. A deficiency causes pellagra which is characterized by rough skin, mouth sores, diarrhea, and mental disorders.

Food Sources: Liver, lean meats, peas, beans, enriched and whole grain cereal products, and fish.

Toxic Side Effects: Liver damage, skin disorders, itching, increased blood sugar, and rapid heart beat.

Pantothenic Acid

Function: Pantothenic acid is needed to support a variety of body functions, including proper growth, development, and maintenance. A deficiency causes headaches, fatigue, poor muscle coordination, nausea, and cramps.

Food Sources: Liver, eggs, white potatoes, sweet potatoes, peas, whole grains (particularly wheat), and peanuts.

Toxic Side Effects: None reported.

Folic Acid—Folacin

Function: Folic acid helps the body to manufacture red blood cells and is essential in normal metabolism (conversion of food into energy). A deficiency of folic acid causes a type of anemia.

Food Sources: Liver, navy beans, nuts, fresh oranges, dark green leafy vegetables, and whole wheat products.

Toxic Side Effects: None reported.

Vitamin B6—Pyridoxine / Pyridoxal / Pyridoxamine

Function: Vitamin B6 has three forms but all are used by the body in the same way. This vitamin is involved mostly in the utilization of protein. As with other vitamins, B6 is essential for the proper growth and maintenance of body functions. Deficiency symptoms include mouth soreness, dizziness, nausea, weight loss, and sometimes severe nervous disturbances.

Food Sources: Liver, whole grain cereals, potatoes, red meats, green vegetables, and yellow corn.

Toxic Side Effects: Liver damage.

Vitamin B12—Cyanocobalamin

Function: Vitamin B12 is necessary for normal development of red blood cells and for proper functioning of all cells, particularly in the bone marrow, nervous system, and intestines. A deficiency causes pernicious anemia, and if the deficiency is prolonged, a degeneration of the spinal cord occurs.

Food Sources: Organ meats, lean meats, fish, milk, eggs, and shellfish. Vitamin B12 is not present to any measurable degree in plants, which means that strict vegetarians should supplement their diets with this vitamin.

Toxic Side Effects: None reported.

Biotin

Function: Once called vitamin H, biotin is actually a member of the B complex vitamins. It's important in the metabolism of carbohydrates, proteins, and fats. Most deficiency symptoms involve mild skin disorders, some anemia, depression, sleeplessness, and muscle pain. A deficiency is extremely rare because bacteria in the intestinal tract produce enough of it to meet the body's demand for it.

Food Sources: Eggs, milk, and meat. "Raw" egg white contains a factor that destroys biotin.

Toxic Side Effects: None reported.

Vitamin C—Ascorbic Acid

Function: This least stable of all the vitamins promotes growth and tissue repair, including the healing of wounds. It aids in tooth and bone formation. When used as a food additive, it acts as a preservative. Lack of vitamin C causes scurvy, one of the oldest known diseases. The signs of scurvy include listlessness, weakness, bleeding, loss of weight, and irritability.

Food Sources: Turnip greens, green pepper, kale, broccoli, mustard greens, citrus fruits, strawberries, tomatoes, and other vegetables.

Toxic Side Effects: Nausea, diarrhea, excessive absorption of iron.

Vitamin D—Calciferol

Function: Vitamin D exists in several forms. The most common are D2 found in plants and D3 found in animals. Vitamin D aids in the absorption of calcium and phosphorous in bone formation.

To accomplish its work, the body—through the liver and the kidneys—converts the vitamin to a hormonelike material. Deficiency of vitamin D causes rickets. The obvious signs are skeletal deformations—bowed legs, deformed spine, "potbelly" appearance, and sometimes flat feet and stunted growth.

Food Sources: Canned and fresh fish (particularly the salt water varieties), egg yolk, and the vitamin D-fortified foods such as milk and margarine.

Toxic Side Effects: Nausea, weight loss, weakness, excessive urination, bone deformities and multiple fractures, kidney damage, growth retardation, and hypertension.

Vitamin K

Function: There are several natural forms of vitamin K, all of which are essential for the clotting of blood. One type, K1, occurs in plants. Another, K2, is formed by bacteria in the intestinal tract. Deficiency of vitamin K causes hemorrhage and liver injury.

Food Sources: Spinach, lettuce, kale, cabbage, cauliflower, liver, and egg yolk.

Toxic Side Effects: The synthetic vitamin K, menadione, is dispensed only by prescription. It may cause irritation of the skin and respiratory tract and could cause anemia because of its ability to break down red blood cells.

Vitamin E—Tocopherol

Function: Vitamin E in humans acts as an antioxidant that helps prevent oxygen from destroying other substances. In other words, vitamin E is a preservative, protecting the activity of other compounds such as vitamin A. No clinical effects have been associated with very low intake of this vitamin in man.

Food Sources: Vegetable oils, beans, eggs, whole grains (the germ), liver, fruits, and vegetables.

Toxic Side Effects: Headache, nausea, fatigue, dizziness, and blurred vision.

APPENDIX D

Health Charts

Keeping track of things like cholesterol, heart rate, blood pressure, body weight, and exercise will keep you more aware of your own personal health state. By maintaining good health and by exercising regularly, you'll not only improve the quality of your life, but will reduce your daily stress to a remarkable degree. A healthier, more fit person will always be able to cope with stress and be more resistant to its effects than someone who doesn't exercise or take care of his or her state of health. Below are some charts that list desirable ranges for various health functions. Compare them with your current state of health and then do something about it.

Blood Pressure Classifications

Diastolic Pressure (lower of the two numbers)

Reading	Category
Less than 85	Normal blood pressure
85 to 89	High normal blood pressure
90 to 104	Mild hypertension
105 to 114	Moderate hypertension
115 or more	Severe hypertension

Systolic Pressure (higher of the two numbers and coupled with a diastolic reading of less than 90)

Reading	Category
Less than 140	Normal blood pressure
140 to 159	Borderline hypertension
160 or more	Hypertension

Note: These categories are for persons 18 years and older. Source: The 1984 "Report of the Joint National Committee on Detection, Evaluation and Treatment of High Blood Pressure."

Cholesterol (in milligrams per deciliter)

Age	Moderate Risk	High Risk
2—19	Over 170	Over 185
20—29	Over 200	Over 220
30—39	Over 220	Over 240
40 and up	Over 240	Over 260

Source: National Institutes of Health consensus conference statement, Lowering Blood Cholesterol, 1984.

Exercise Pulse Rates

Age	Target Zone
20	120—150
25	117—146
30	114—142
35	111—138
40	108—135
45	105—131
50	102—127
55	99—123
60	96—120
65	93—116
70	90—113

Note: "Target zone" is the pulse or heart rate in beats per minute. Exercise that sustains that target level for 30 minutes should be undertaken at least three times a week. Persons over 40 who have not been exercising regularly should consult a doctor before starting such a program. Source: Exercise and Your Heart, National Heart, Lung and Blood Institute.

Desirable Body Weight Ranges

Men

Height	Small Frame	Medium Frame	Large Frame
5′1″	105–114	115–124	125–134
5′2″	108–117	118–127	128–137
5′3″	111–120	121–130	131–140
5′4″	114–124	125–135	136–146
5′5″	117–127	128–138	139–149
5′6″	121–131	132–142	143–153
5′7″	125–136	137–147	148–158
5′8″	129–140	141–152	153–164
5′9″	133–144	145–156	157–168
5′10″	137–148	149–160	161–172
5′11″	141–152	153–164	165–176
6′0″	145–157	158–170	171–183
6′1″	149–161	162–174	175–187
6′2″	153–165	166–178	179–192
6′3″	157–169	170–182	183–195

Women

Height	Small Frame	Medium Frame	Large Frame
4′10″	92–101	102–111	112–121
4′11″	95–104	105–114	115–124
5′0″	98–107	108–117	118–127
5′1″	101–110	111–120	121–130
5′2″	104–113	114–123	124–133
5′3″	107–117	118–128	129–139
5′4″	110–121	122–132	133–143
5′5″	114–124	125–135	136–146
5′6″	118–128	129–139	140–150
5′7″	122–132	133–143	144–154
5′8″	126–136	137–147	148–158
5′9″	130–141	142–153	154–164
5′10″	134–145	146–157	158–169

Source: Adapted from 1985 Dietary Guidelines for Americans, U.S. Department of Health and Human Services.

Exercise Energy Expenditures

Activity	Calories per hour
Lying quietly	80–100
Sitting quietly	85–105
Standing quietly	100–120
Walking slowly, 2 1/2 mph	210–230
Walking quickly, 4 mph	315–345
Light work such as ballroom dancing; cleaning house; office work; shopping, etc.	125–310
Moderate work such as cycling, 9 mph; jogging, 6 mph; tennis; scrubbing floors; weeding garden, etc.	315–480
Hard work such as aerobics; basketball; chopping wood; cross-country skiing; running, 7 mph; shoveling snow; spading garden; swimming, etc.	480–625

Note: These are energy expenditures by a healthy adult weighing about 150 pounds. Source: Adapted from 1985 Dietary Guidelines for Americans, U.S. Department of Health and Human Services.

BIBLIOGRAPHY

Abush, R. and Burkhead, E.J. 1984. Job stress in midlife working women: relationships among personality type, job characteristics and job tension. J. Couns. Psychol. 31: 36.

Agras, W.S. 1980. Relaxation training twenty-four hour blood pressure reductions. Arch. Gen. Psychiat. 37:859.

Ahlburg, D.A. and Schapiro, M.O. 1983. The darker side of unemployment. Hosp. and Comm. Psychiat. 34:389.

Alkus, S. and Padesky. 1983. Special problems of police officers: stress-related issues and interventions. Couns. Psychol. 11:55.

Anderson, D.E. 1984. Interactions of stress, salt, and blood pressure. Ann. Rev. Physiol. 46:143.

Aneshensel, C.S. and Stone, J.D. 1982. Stress and depression. Arch. Gen. Psychiat. 39:1392.

Archer, J. 1986. Stress management: evaluating a preventive approach for college students. J. Am. Coll. Health. 34: 157.

Aro, S. 1981. Stress, morbidity, and health related behavior. Scand. J. of Soc. Med. Suppl. 5:1.

Arensault, A. and Shimon, D. 1983. The role of personality, occupation, and organization in understanding the relationship between job stress, performance, and absenteeism. J. Occup. Psychol. 56:227.

Axelrod, J. and Reisine, T.D. 1984. Stress Hormones: their interaction and regulation. Science. 224:452.

Averill, J.R. 1973. Personal control over adversive stimuli and its relationship to stress. Psychol. Bull. 40:196.

Backer, G. et al. 1983. Behavior, stress, and psychosocial traits as risk factors. Prev. Med. 12:32.

Bahlmann, J. et al. 1982. Stress-induced changes of the venous circulation. Contr. Nephrol. 30:43.

Baker, G.H. 1984. Stress, cortisol, and lymphocyte subpopulations. Lancet. 8376:574.

Bartz, C. et al. 1986. Burnout among intensive care nurses. Res. Nurs. Health. 9:147.

Baum, A. et al. 1983. Emotional, behavioral, and physiological effects of chronic stress at Three Mile Island. J. Consult. Clin. Psychol. 51:565.

Beels, C.C. and McFarlane W.R. 1982. Family treatments of schizophrenia: background and state of the art. Hosp. and Comm. Psychiat. 33:541.

Benson, H. et al. 1974. The relaxation response. Psychiatry. 37:37.

Benson, H. 1977. Systemic hypertension and the relaxation response. N. Eng. J. Med. 296:1152.

Bergen, G.T. and Bartol, C.R. 1983. Stress in rural law enforcement. Percep. Mot. Skills. 56:957.

Bergman, L.R. and Magnusson, D. 1986. Type A Behavior: A longitudinal study from childhood to adulthood. Psychosom. Med. 48:134.

Berkman, L.F. 1983. The assessment of social networks and social support in the elderly. J. Am. Geriatr. Soc. 31: 743.

Bidzinska, E.J. 1984. Stress factors in affective diseases. Br. J. Psychiat. 144:161.

Birley, J.L.T. and Brown, G.W. 1970. Crises and life changes preceding the onset or relapse of acute schizophrenia. Br. J. Psychiat. 116:327.

Bland, R.C. and Orn, H. 1981. Schizophrenia: sociocultural factors. Can. J. Psychol. 26:186.

Blue, F.R. 1979. Aerobic exercise as a treatment for moderate depression. Percep. Mot. Skills. 48:228.

Borysenko, M. and Borysenko, J. 1982. Stress, behavior, and immunity: animal models and mediating mechanisms. Gen. Hosp. Psychiat. 4:59.

Brady, J.P. 1984. Social skills training for psychiatric patients, I: Concepts, methods, and clinical results. Am. J. Psychiat. 141:333.

Brodsky, C.M. 1984. Long-term work stress. Psychosomatics. 25:361.

Brown, G.W. et al. 1973. Life events and psychiatric disorders. Psychol. Med. 3:74.

Brown, J.D. and Lawton, M. 1986. Stress and well-being in adolescence: the moderating role of physical exercise. J. Human Stress. 12:125.

Brown, S.D. 1980. Coping skills training: an evaluation of a psychoeducational program in a community mental health setting. J. Couns. Psychiat. 27:340.

————— 1983. Coping skills training: attitude toward mental illness, depression, and quality of life 1 year later. J. Couns. Psychiat. 30:117.

Burchfield, S.R. 1979. The stress response: A new perspective. Psychosom. Med. 41:661.

Burrows, T.M. 1982. Stress and the medical profession: doctors are people too. J. Holistic Med. 4:68.

Chaisson, M. et al. 1984. Treating the depressed elderly. J. Psychosoc. Nurs. 22:5.

Chisholm, R.F. et al. 1983. The nature and predictors of job related tension in a crisis situation: reactions of nuclear workers to the Three Mile Island accident. Acad. Manag. J. 26:385.

Clarke, M. 1984. Stress and coping: constructs for nursing. J. Adv. Nurs. 9:3.

Cleary, P.D. and Houts, P.S. 1984. The psychological impact of the Three Mile Island Incident. J. Human Stress. 10: 28.

Cohen, C.I. et al. 1986. Assessment of stress-buffering effects of social networks on psychological symptoms in an inner-city elderly population. Am. J. Comm. Psychol. 14:75.

Cohen, M.R. et al. 1983. The role of the endogenous opioid system in the human stress response. Psychiat. Clin. N. Am. 6:457.

Cohen, S. et al. 1986. Social skills and the stress-protective role of social support. J. Pers. Soc. Psychol. 50: 963.

Cooper, C.L. 1983. Identifying stressors at work: recent research developments. J. Psychosom. Res. 27:369.

Cooper, C.L. and Melbuish, A. 1984. Executive stress and health. J. Occup. Med. 26:99.

Cooper, C.L. et al. 1986. A survey of stress at work. J. Soc. Occup. Med. 36:71.

Couch, J.R. and Diamond, S. 1983. Status migrainous: causative and therapeutic aspects. Headache. 23:94.

Coyne, J.C. et al. 1981. Depression and coping in stressful episodes. J. Abnorm. Psychol. 90:439.

─────────── 1986. Going beyond social support: the role of social relationships in adaptation. J. Consult. Clin. Psychol. 54:454.

Crowther, J.H. 1983. Stress management training and relaxation imagery in the treatment of essential hypertension. J. Behav. Med. 6:169.

Davis, A.J. 1984. Stress. Am. J. Nurs. 84:365.

Dawson, D. 1986. Ten 'A' commandments from the Good Health Symposium. Practitioner. 230:516.

DeLongis, A. et al. 1982. Relationship of daily hassle, uplifts, and major life events to health status. Health Psychology. 1:119.

Denton, D.A. et al. 1984. Stress, ACTH, salt intake, and high blood pressure. Clin. Exp. Hypert. 6:403.

Dignam, J.T. et al. 1986. Occupational stress, social support, and burnout among correctional officers. Am. J. Comm. Psychol. 14(2):177.

Dimsdale, J.E. and Moss, J. 1980. Plasma catecholamines in stress and exercise. J.A.M.A. 243:340.

Dimsdale, J.E. and Herd, A. 1982. Variability of plasma lipids in response to emotional arousal. Psychosom. Med. 44:413.

Dorian, B.J. et al. 1982. Aberrations in lymphocyte subpopulations and functions during psychological stress. Clin. Exp. Immunol. 50:132.

Egan, K.J. et al. 1983. The impact of psychological distress on the control of hypertension. J. Hum. Stress. 9(4):4.

Emery, P.E. 1983. Adolescent depression and suicide. Adolescence. 18:245.

Emrich, H.M. and Millan, M.J. 1982. Stress reactions and endorphinergic systems. J. Psychosom. Med. 26:101.

Featherstone, H.J. and Beitman, B.D. 1983. "Daily" common migraine: psychosocial predictors of outcomes of medical therapy. Headache. 23:110.

Feinson, M.C. 1986. The distribution of distress among elders. J. Gerontol. 41(2):225.

Felser, J.M. and Raff, M.J. 1983. Infectious diseases and aging: Immunologic perspectives. J. Am. Geriatr. Soc. 31:802.

Francis, K.T. et al. 1983. Perceived sources of stress and coping strategies in allied health students: a model. J. Allied Health. 12:262.

Friedman, M. et al. 1958. Changes in the serum cholesterol and blood clotting time in men subjected to cyclic variation of occupational stress. Circulation. 17:852.

Friedman, M.J. and Bennet, P.L. 1977. Depression and hypertension. Psychosom. Med. 39:134.

Gaines, J. and Jermier, J.M. 1983. Emotional exhaustion in a high stress organization. Acad. Manag. J. 26:567.

Ganster, D.C. et al. 1982. Managing organizational stress: a field experiment. J. Appl. Psychol. 67:533.

─────── 1986. Role of social support in the experience of stress at work. J. Appl. Psychol. 71(1): 102.

Gaudin, J.M. and Pollance, L. 1983. Social networks, stress, and child abuse. Child. Youth Serv. Rev. 5:91.

Gelenberg, A.J. et al. 1983. Tyrosine for depression. J. Psychiat. Res. 17:175.

Gillman, M.A. and Lichtigfed, F.J. 1983. The opioid system in anorexia nervosa. Am. J. Psychiatry. 140:371.

Glass, D.C. 1977. Stress, behavior patterns, and coronary disease. Am. Scientist. 65:177.

Gmelch, W.H. 1983. Stress for success: how to optimize your performance. Theory into Pract. 22:7.

Goldfield, M. and Trier, C. 1974. Effectiveness of relaxation as an active coping skill. J. Abnorm. Psychol. 83:348.

Goldstein, D.S. 1983. Plasma catecholamines and essential hypertension. 5:86.

Gottschalk, L.A. 1983. Vulnerability to stress. Am. J. Psychother. 37:5.

Harris, L. et al. 1974. The myth and reality of aging in America. Washington, D.C.: National Council on Aging.

Hart, K.E. and Jamieson, J.L. 1983. Type A behavior and cardiovascular recovery from a psychosocial stressor. J. Human Stress. 9:18.

Haynes, S. et al. 1974. Relaxation treatment of insomnia. Behav. Therapy. 5:555.

Heilbrum, A.B. 1986. Type A behavior, cognitive defense, and stress. Psychol. Rep. 58(2):447.

Hendin, A. 1983. Psychotherapy for Vietnam veterans with posttraumatic stress disorder. Am. J. Psychother. 37:86.

─────── 1984. Combat never ends: the paranoid adaptation to post-traumatic stress. Am. J. Psychother. 38:121.

Henry, J.P. 1986. Mechanisms by which stress can lead to coronary heart disease. Postgrad. Med. J. 62:687.

Herbert, B. 1983. The relaxation response: its subjective and objective historical precedents and physiology. Trends in Neurosciences. 6:281.

Herd, J.A. 1984. Cardiovascular response to stress in men. Ann. Rev. Physiol. 46:177.

Hoiberg, A. et al. 1984. The traumatic aftereffects of collision at sea. Am. J. Psychiat. 141:70.

Holahan, C.J. et al. 1986. Personality, coping, and family resources in stress resistance: a longitudinal study. J. Pers. Soc. Psychol. 51(2):389.

Holm, J.E. 1986. The role of stress in recurrent tension headache. Headache. 26(4):160.

Houts, P.S. et al. 1984. Utilization of medical care following the Three Mile Island crisis. Am. J. Pub.Health. 74:140.

Howard, C.E. et al. 1986. A comparison of methods for reducing stress among dental students. J. Dent. Educ. 50(9):542.

Howard, J.H. et al. 1986. Personality (hardiness) as a moderator of job stress and coronary risk in Type A individuals: a longitudinal study. J. Behav. Med. 9(3):229.

Irvine, M.J. et al. 1986. Relaxation and stress management in the treatment of essential hypertension. J. Psychosom. Res. 30(4):437.

Jacobs, T.J. and Charles, E. 1980. Life events and the occurrence of cancer in children. Psychosom. Med. 42:11.

Jamal, M. 1984. Job stress and job performance controversy: an empirical assessment. Org. Behav. Hum. Perform. 33:1.

Jasnoski, M. et al. 1981. Exercise, changes in aerobic capacity, and changes in self-perceptions: an experimental investigation. J. Res. Personal. 15:460.

Jemmott, J.B. et al. 1983. Academic stress, power motivation and decrease in secretion rate of salivary secretory immunoglobulin A. Lancet. 8339:1400.

Jemmott, J.B. and Locke, S.E. 1984. Psychosocial factors, immunological mediation, and human susceptibility to infectious disease: how much do we know? Psychol. Bull. 95:78.

Jenkins, C.D. 1966. Components of the coronary-prone behavior pattern. J. Chron. Dis. 19:599.

Joffe, R.T. and Offord, D.R. 1983. Suicidal behavior in childhood. Can. J. Psychol. 28:57.

Johnson, C.L. 1983. Dyadic family relations and social support. Gerontologist. 23:377.

Johnston, D.W. 1985. Psychological intervention in cardiovascular disease. J. Psychosom. Res. 29:447.

Jonsson, A. and Hansson, L. 1977. Prolonged exposure to a stressful stimulus (noise) as a cause of raised blood pressure in man. Lancet. 8001:86.

Kahn, M. et al. 1968. Treatment of insomnia by relaxation training. J. Abnorm. Psychol. 73:556.

Kasl, S.V. et al. 1968. Changes in serum uric acid and cholesterol levels in men undergoing job loss. J.A.M.A. 206:7.

Kobasa, S.C. et al. 1979. Who stays healthy under stress? J. Occup. Med. 21:595.

_____ 1981. Personality and constitution as mediators in the stress-illness relationship. J. Health Soc. Behav. 22:368.

——————— 1982. Hardiness and health. J. Personal. Soc. Psychol. 42:168.

——————— 1982. Personality and exercise as buffers in the stress-illness relationship. J. Behav. Med. 5:391.

Kornitzer, M. et al. 1986. How does stress exert its effects—smoking, diet and obesity, physical activity? Postgrad. Med. J. 62:695.

Krakowski, A.J. 1982. Stress and the practice of medicine. Stressors, stresses, and strains. Psychother. Psychosom. 38:11.

Krause, N. 1985. Stress, control beliefs, and psychological distress: the problem of response bias. J. Hum. Stress. 11(1):11.

——————— 1986. Social support, stress, and well-being among older adults. J. Gerontol. 41(4):512.

Kuo, W.H. et al. 1986. Social networking, hardiness, and immigrant's mental health. J. Health Soc. Behav. 27(2): 133.

Lawton, M.P. 1983. Environment and other determinants of well-being in older people. Gerontologist. 23:349.

Lewis, C.E. 1984. Feeling bad: exploring sources of distress among pre-adolescent children. Am. J. Publ. Health. 74: 117.

Lieberman, P.B. and Strauss, J.S. 1984. The recurrence of mania: environmental factors and medical treatment. Am. J. Psychiat. 141:77.

Light, K.C. et al. 1983. Psychosocial stress induces sodium and fluid retention in men at high risk for hypertension. Science. 220:429.

Linden, W. and Feuerstein, M. 1981. Essential hypertension and social coping behavior. J. Hum. Stress. 7:28.

Lloyd, C.L. 1980. Life events and depressive disorder reviewed. Arch. Gen. Psychiat. 37:541.

Locke, S.E. 1982. Stress, adaptation, and immunity: studies in humans. Gen. Hosp. Psychiat. 4:49.

Locke, S.E. and Heisel, S.J. 1977. The influence of stress and emotions on the human immune response. Biofeedback and Self-Regulation. 2:320.

Lovallo, W.R. et al. 1986. Work pressure and the Type A behavior pattern exam stress in male medical students. Psychosom. Med. 48(2):125.

Lowenthal, M.F. 1964. Social isolation and mental illness in old age. Am. Sociol. Rev. 29:54.

MacBride, A. 1983. Burnout: Possible? Probable? Preventable? Can. Ment. Health. 31:2.

Maloney, J.P. 1982. Job stress and its consequences on a group of intensive care and nonintensive care nurses. Adv. Nurs. Sci. 4:31.

Maloney, J.P. and Bartz, C. 1983. Stress tolerant people: intensive care nurses compared with nonintensive care nurses. Heart and Lung. 12:389.

Marmot, M.G. 1986. Does stress cause heart attacks? Postgrad. Med. J. 62:686.

Martin, I. 1970. Progressive relaxation facilitated. Behav. Res. and Therapy. 8:217.

Marx, J.L. 1980. Natural killer cells help defend the body. Science. 210:624.

Maslach, C. and Jackson, S.E. 1977. Lawyer burnout. Barrister. 5:52.

McCall, M.W. and Lombardo, M.M. 1983. What makes a top executive? Psychol. Today. 17:26.

McCann, I.L. and Homes, D.S. 1984. Influence of aerobic exercise on depression. J. Pers. Soc. Psychol. 46:1142.

McClure, G.M.G. 1984. Recent trends in suicide among the young. Br. J. Psychiat. 144:134.

McDermott, D. 1984. Professional burnout and its relation to job characteristics, satisfaction, and control. J. Hum. Stress. 10(2):79.

Michaels, E. 1982. Pets and the elderly: a therapeutic friendship. Can. Med. Assoc. J. 127:70.

Minkler, M.A. et al. 1983. Supportive exchange: an exploration of the relationship between social contacts and perceived health status in the elderly. Arch. Gerontol. and Geriatr. 2:179.

Mintz, N. and Schwartz, D. 1964. Urban ecology and psychosis: community factors in the incidence of schizophrenia and manic-depression among Italians in greater Boston. Int. J. Soc. Psychiat. 10:101.

Morris, R.J. 1973. Shaping relaxation in an unrelaxed client. J. Behav. Therapy and Exp. Psychiat. 4:353.

Murphy, L.R. 1983. A comparison of relaxation methods for reducing stress in nursing personnel. Hum. Factors. 25: 431.

Myers, J.K. et al. 1977. Life events and psychiatric impairment. J. Nerv. and Ment. Dis. 152:149.

Newbrough, A. 1983. Twelve steps towards revitalization for teachers. Education. 103:270.

Newman, J.P. 1986. Gender, life strains, and depression. J. Health Soc. Behav. 27(2):193.

Nilsson, L.V. 1983. Personality changes in the aged. Acta Psychiat. Scand. 68:202.

O'Hara, M. et al. 1983. Postpartum depression: a role for social network and life stress variables. J. Nerv. and Ment. Dis. 171:336.

Panconesi, E. 1984. Stress and skin disease: psychosomatic dermatology. Clin. Dermatol. 2(4):viii.

Parkes, K.R. 1982. Occupational stress among student nurses: a natural experiment. J. Appl. Psychol. 67:784.

Paykel, E.S. et al. 1969. Life events and depression. Arch. Gen. Psychiat. 21:753.

Pendleton, L. and Tasto, D. 1976. Effects of metronome induced relaxation and progressive muscle relaxation on insomnia. Behav. Res. and Therapy. 14:165.

Perini, C. et al. 1982. Personality and adrenergic factors in essential hypertension. Contr. Nephrol. 30:64.

Perris, H. 1984. Life events and personality characteristics in depression. Acta Psychiat. Scand. 69:350.

Pilowsky, I. et al. 1973. Hypertension and personality. Psychiat. Med. 35:50.

Pines, M. 1980. Psychological hardiness: the role of challenge to health. Psychol. Today. 14(7):34.

Podell, R.N. 1983. Nutritional precursers and the treatment of depression. Postgrad. Med. 73:99.

Polakoff, P.L. 1983. How the well cope with potential illness. Occup. Health and Safety. 52:48.

Rabkin, J.G. and Struening. 1976. Life events, stress, and illness. Science. 194:1013.

Rapelje, D.H. 1983. Elderly and pets are meant for each other. Dim. Health Serv. 11:11.

Riccio, A.C. 1983. On coping with the stresses of teaching. Theory into Pract. 22:43.

Riscalla, L.M. 1982. The influence of psychological factors on the immune system. Med. Hypoth. 9:331.

Rootman, I. and Sydiaha, D. 1969. Ethnic groups within communities: a comparable study of the expression and definition of mental illness. Psychiat. Quart. 43:131.

Rose, R.L. and Veiga, J.F. 1984. Assessing the sustained effects of a stress management intervention on anxiety and locus of control. Acad. Manag. J. 27:190.

Rose, R.M. 1980. Endocrine responses to stressful psychological events. Psychiat. Clin. N. Amer. 3:251.

Roth, D.L. and Holmes, D.S. 1985. Influence of physical fitness in determining the impact of stressful life events in physical and psychological health. Psychosom. Med. 47:164.

Roth, S. et al. 1986. Approach, avoidance, and coping with stress. Am. Psychol. 41(7):813.

Russell, R. et al. 1976. Progressive relaxation training: a procedural note. Behav. Therapy. 7:566.

Schilling, D.J. and Poppen, R. 1983. Behavioral relaxation training and assessment. J. Behav. Therapy and Exp. Psychol. 14:99.

Schotte, D.E. and Clum, G.A. 1982. Suicide ideation in a college population. J. Couns. and Clin. Psychiat. 50:690.

Selye, H. 1936. The alarm reaction. Can. Med. Assoc. J. 34: 706.

——————— 1937. Studies on adaptation. Endocrinology. 21: 169.

——————— 1946. The General Adaptation Syndrome and the diseases of adaptation. J. Clin. Endocrinol. 6:117.

Severtsen, B. et al. 1986. Effects of meditation and aerobic exercise on EEG patterns. J. Neurosci. Nurs. 18(4):206.

Shekelle, R.B. et al. 1981. Psychological depression and 17-year risk of death from cancer. Psychosom. Med. 43:117.

Sklar, L.S. and Anisman, H. 1981. Stress and cancer. Psychol. Bull. 89(3):369.

Smith, J.R. et al. 1983. On health and disorder in Vietnam veterans. Amer. J. Orthopsychiat. 53:27.

Southam. M.A. et al. 1982. Relaxation training: blood pressure lowering during the working day. Arch. Gen. Psychiat. 39:715.

Stensrud, R. and Stensrud, K. 1983. Coping skills training: a systematic approach to stress management counseling. Personnel and Guidance J. 62:214.

Steptoe, A. 1983. Stress, helplessness, and control: the implications of laboratory studies. J. Psychosom. Res. 27:361.

Stout, C.W. and Bloom, L.J. 1981. Type A behavior and upper respiratory infections. J. Hum. Stress. 8:4.

Stuart, J.C. and Brown, B.M. 1981. The relationship of stress and coping ability to incidence of diseases and accidents. J. Psychosom. Res. 25:255.

Svensson, J. and Theorell, T. 1983. Life events and elevated blood pressure in young men. J. Psychosom. Res. 27:445

Szabo, S. et al. 1983. Occupational stress: understanding, recognition, and prevention. Experientia. 39:1057.

Tasto, D. and Hinkle, J. 1973. Muscle relaxation and treatment for tension headaches. Behav. Res. and Therapy. 11: 347.

Thomas, S.A. et al. 1984. Blood pressure and heart rate changes in children when they read aloud in school. Publ. Health Rep. 99:77.

Thomas, S.C. 1981. Will it hurt if I can control it? A complex answer to a simple question. Psychol. Bull. 90: 89.

Thorts, P.A. 1986. Social support as a coping assistance. J. Consult. Clin. Psychol. 54(4):416.

Trevison, M. et al. 1983. Nervous tension and serum cholesterol: findings from the Chicago coronary prevention evaluation program. J. Hum. Stress. 9:12.

Turner, R.J. 1981. Social support as a contingency in psychological well-being. J. Health and Soc. Behav. 22: 357.

Udelman, D.L. 1982. Stress and immunity. Psychother. Psychosom. 37:176.

Verrier, R.L. and Lown, B. 1984. Behavioral stress and cardiacarrhythmias. Ann. Rev. Physiol. 46:155.

Wallace, R.K. and Benson, H. 1972. The physiology of meditation. Sci. Am. 226:84.

Warren, S. et al. 1982. Emotional stress and the development of multiple sclerosis: case-control evidence of a relationship. J. Chron. Dis. 35:821.

Williams, C.C. 1983. The mental foxhole: the Vietnam veteran's search for meaning. Am. J. Orthopsychiat. 53:4.

INDEX

B

C

H

I

M

Give Copies to Friends, Loved Ones, Business Associates, Doctors

ORDER FORM

YES, I want to attain a stress free future! Send me the books marked below.

☐ Please send_____hardcover copies of *Breaking the Stress Habit: A Modern Guide to One-Minute Stress Management* at $16.95 + $2 per book shipping and handling.

☐ Please send_____paperback copies of *Breaking the Stress Habit: A Modern Guide to One-Minute Stress Management* at $9.95 + $2 per book shipping and handling.

(North Carolina residents should add 5% state sales tax. Canadian orders must be accompanied by a postal money order in U.S. funds.) Please allow 30 days for delivery.

Name_____

Phone (____)_____

Address _____

City/State/Zip _____

Here's my check, made out to Carolina Press, in the amount of

$_____ Mail to: Carolina Press, Box 24906, Winston-Salem, NC 27114.

QUANTITY ORDERS INVITED

For quantity discount prices or special UPS handling, please call 919-768-9180.